Exceptional Cars
Ford GT40 Mk II

Porter Press International

Also published by Porter Press International

The Jaguar Portfolio
Ultimate E-type – The Competition Cars
Jaguar E-type – The Definitive History (2nd edition)
Original Jaguar XK (3rd edition)
Jaguar Design – A Story of Style
Saving Jaguar

Original Scrapbooks
Stirling Moss Scrapbook 1929-1954
Stirling Moss Scrapbook 1955
Stirling Moss Scrapbook 1956-1960
Stirling Moss Scrapbook 1961
Graham Hill Scrapbook 1929-1966
Murray Walker Scrapbook
Martin Brundle Scrapbook
Barry Cryer Comedy Scrapbook

Great Cars series
No. 1 – Jaguar Lightweight E-type – the autobiography of 4 WPD
No. 2 – Porsche 917 – the autobiography of 917-023
No. 3 – Jaguar D-type – the autobiography of XKD 504
No. 4 – Ferrari 250GT SWB – the autobiography of 2119 GT
No. 5 – Maserati 250F – the autobiography of 2528
No. 6 – ERA – the autobiography of R4D
No. 7 – Ferrari 250GTO – the autobiography of 4153 GT
No. 8 – Jaguar Lightweight E-type – the autobiography of 49 FXN
No. 9 – Jaguar C-type – the autobiography of XKC 051
No. 10 – Lotus 18 – the autobiography of Stirling Moss's '912'
No. 11 – Ford GT40 – the autobiography of 1075

Exceptional Cars series
No. 1 - Iso Bizzarrini - the remarkable history of A3/C 0222
No. 2 - Jaguar XK120 - the remarkable history of JWK 651
No. 3 - Ford GT 40 - the remarkable history of 1016

Porter Profiles
No. 1 - Austin Healey - the story of DD 300

Deluxe leather-bound, signed, limited editions with slipcases are available for most titles.
Books available from retailers or signed copies direct from the publisher.
To order simply phone +44 (0)1584 781588, fax +44 (0)1584 781630, visit the website or email sales@porterpress.co.uk

Keep up-to-date with news about current books and new releases at:
www.porterpress.co.uk

Exceptional Cars

Ford GT40 Mk II

The remarkable history of 1016

Mark Cole

Porter Press International

©Mark Cole

All rights reserved. No part of this publication may be reproduced, stored in a retrieval system or transmitted, in any form or by any means, electronic, mechanical, photocopying, recording or otherwise, without prior permission in writing from the publisher

First published in January 2018
Reprinted August 2018

978-1-907085-64-2

Published by
Porter Press International Ltd

Hilltop Farm, Knighton-on-Teme, Tenbury Wells, WR15 8LY, UK
Tel: +44 (0)1584 781588   Fax: +44 (0)1584 781630
sales@porterpress.co.uk
www.porterpress.co.uk

Edited by Ray Hutton
Design & Layout by Andrew Garman

Printed by Gomer Press Ltd

COPYRIGHT

We have made every effort to trace and acknowledge copyright holders and we apologise in advance for any unintentional omission. We would be pleased to insert the appropriate acknowledgement in any subsequent edition.

Contents

Introduction 7

Ford and Le Mans 8

1 Ford versus Ferrari 10
2 The birth of the GT40 14
3 Shelby takes control 24
4 Heading to victory 30

The story of 1016 34

5 Preparing for battle 36
6 Daytona 24 Hours 40
7 Sebring 12 Hours 50
8 Le Mans 24 Hours 58
9 Daytona 24 Hours 76
10 Le Mans Test Weekend 86
11 Postscript to 1967 90

The Second Life of 1016 94

12 Renewed and back on track 96
13 Photo Gallery 114

Acknowledgements 126
Index 127

Introduction

Henry Ford had a dream that every American would be able to afford his or her own car. His grandson Henry Ford II also had a dream, that Ford would win the Le Mans 24 Hours, and sell even more cars. He first tried to do it by buying Ferrari, but when his wooing was rebuffed, he got together the world's finest race car builders, engineers and drivers, and threw money at them to realise that dream.

It took two years longer than he had intended, but it eventually all came good in June 1966, when Ford GT40 MK IIs crossed the Le Mans finish-line in a 1-2-3 echelon, ending Ferrari's long stranglehold on the world's most famous race. Fords were to repeat that success over the next three years, although after the second year 'The Deuce' had moved on to other things, and it was left to Briton John Wyer and his team to bring home the spoils.

The car which finished third in 1966, P/1016, arguably was one of the most important Ford GT40s to be produced. Destined for Holman & Moody as a race car, it was shipped by Ford Advanced Vehicles from Slough to Shelby American in Los Angeles to be upgraded to Mk II specification.

But before delivery to Holman & Moody, it was used as Ford's pre-season test car during January 1966, running at Sebring. The data collected and modifications made during those eight days were crucial to Ford's clean sweep at Le Mans.

1016 also played a vital supporting role in the 1966 race; it was later revealed that team orders from the top had held it back, in case anything happened to the two Shelby Mk IIs ahead. It had a short competition life, competing in only four races, but was used for further development work for the defence of Ford's crown. Following the 1967 Le Mans Test weekend, where it ran fourth fastest ahead of the new Mk IV, it was retired and passed on to Harrah's Motor Museum in Nevada. But it was then to start a new career in historic racing and at *concours* gatherings, and is still going strong, more than 50 years later.

This is the story not only of that extraordinary car, today restored to the specification in which it finished Le Mans and owned by Claude Nahum, but also of the whole of Ford's four-year programme, which eventually netted two victories in the 24 Hours. It was at a massive cost in both dollars - $22 million - and in human life. Politics and intrigue also feature, as in any good story. Only this one is true.

● Back where it belongs. The Ford GT40 was built to win Le Mans and 1016 played its part, with third place in the victorious trio in 1966. Present owner Claude Nahum has been a regular competitor in the Le Mans Classic since acquiring the car in 2004.

Part 1
Ford and Le Mans

The Ford GT40 makes its debut at Le Mans in 1964: Richard Attwood (12) leads Bruce McLaren through the Esses. Attwood's car caught fire and McLaren's broke its gearbox, as did the third Ford of Richie Ginther and Masten Gregory.
The Revs Institute for Automotive Research/Eric della Faille

Of all the countless motor races since the dawn of motoring, none has captured the imagination more than the Le Mans 24 Hours.

The first-ever Grand Prix – the French - was held outside the ancient city of Le Mans in 1906. Two years later, Wilbur Wright made his first aeroplane flights outside the United States from what we now know as the Mulsanne straight. And in 1923, the first 24-hour endurance race on public roads started an event which has become a legend.

There have now been 85 editions of *Les 24 Heures du Mans*, the race every manufacturer wants to win. Its roll of honour includes Bentley, Jaguar, Aston Martin, Ferrari, Renault, Porsche, Audi and Ford.

This is the story of the Blue Oval's battle to win this most prestigious of events, at a time when Ford was re-establishing itself as a force in the world of motorsport after lean years of restriction by American road safety resolutions. In the 1960s Henry Ford II tried to get a head start by buying Ferrari; he was rebuffed, and had to begin his Le Mans programme from scratch. It cost Ford $22 million, but the cars won it, not once, but four times. In marketing terms, it was worth every cent…

Chapter 1
Ford versus Ferrari

In the early 1960s - the era of the Beach Boys, the Beatles and the Mini - Ford was the world's second-largest motor manufacturer. Chairman Henry Ford II had taken it public in 1956, although he was careful to keep 40 per cent of its shares within the family.

But Ford's image had become jaded and middle-aged, an image not helped by the 1957 Detroit Safety Resolution, an Automobile Manufacturers of America (General Motors, Ford and Chrysler) agreement with Congress to cease all racing activities, and to provide good, staid, cars and to keep well away from anything suggesting power and performance.

This went against Henry Ford I's ethos; he had written in his 1923 autobiography, 'The automobile had passed from the initial stage where the fact that it could run at all was enough, to the stage where it had to show speed. I designed a two-cylinder enclosed engine of a more compact type than I had before used, fitted it into a skeleton chassis, found that I could make speed, and arranged a race with Alexander Winton of Cleveland. We met on the Grosse Point track at Detroit (in October 1901). I beat him. That was my first race, and it brought advertising of the only kind that people cared to read.'

Nonetheless, in June 1957 Ford sold its NASCAR racing assets – race cars, Charlotte race shop and equipment – to engineer John Holman and driver Ralph Moody for just $15,000, to show its support for the Safety Resolution. Its AMA partners also complied, at least to start with.

Soon Pontiac, a GM subsidiary, started to race again, covertly funding NASCAR teams, and was not slow in crowing about its 1961 Daytona 500 success. Chevrolet too was funding competition, through a shadow 'marine engine' programme.

GM had been producing its iconic Chevrolet Corvette since 1953, and vice-president Bill Mitchell had no intention of letting the Corvette racing programme drop, so continued to design and build racing 'Vettes in secret. By 1962, his second-generation Corvette Stingray had become a cult car, while Ford was losing its market share with its 'smooth, quiet, living rooms on wheels' as Cobra Daytona coupe designer Peter Brock described them: Falcons, Fairlanes and Galaxies.

The two GM marques won 41 of 52 NASCAR races in 1961, and Henry Ford II and his new Ford Division head Lee Iacocca could only look on as the Corvette also dominated American road racing, and European manufacturers Jaguar, Aston Martin and Ferrari took honours year after year in the world's greatest race - the Le Mans 24 Hours. Success in the French classic did wonders for their car sales worldwide.

Ford's moratorium did not, however, stop others such as Californian tuner Carroll Shelby and Lola's Eric Broadley from using Ford's 4.7 litre and 4.2 litre V8 engines for their own race cars. The Shelby Cobra was based on the British AC Ace, and soon became the benchmark for GT racing. And Lola, like Lotus, was earning a reputation for innovative British competition car design.

Enough was enough, said Iacocca, and in June 1962, Henry Ford II – although chairman of the Detroit Safety Resolution committee - withdrew from the now dead-in-the-water agreement, giving the go-ahead for Ford to officially re-enter NASCAR with Holman & Moody.

Ferrari dominance at Le Mans. The factory 250 Testa Rossa 61 won in 1961, driven by Phil Hill and Olivier Gendebien. The second American after Luigi Chinetti (1949) to win the 24 Hours, Hill did it three times - in 1958, 1961 and 1962 - before joining the Ford challenge in 1964.
The Revs Institute for Automotive Research/George Phillips

Ford versus Ferrari

The model used was the Galaxie 500, the engine a Ford 427cu.in. V8. Led by Tiny Lund, the Blue Oval cars swept the 1963 Daytona 500 with a 1-2-3-4-5.

Also in 1962, with an eye on an increasingly youthful car market, Iacocca took the decision launch a rival to the Corvette, the Mustang, and to bring Ford back into motorsport as a whole, launching a programme which he called Total Performance.

Ford re-entered the sport globally, under motorsport boss Jacque Passino, with a wide sweep across NASCAR, Formula 1, rallying, touring car racing and the World Sports Car Championship, which then included both the Le Mans 24 Hours and Daytona Continental races.

By May 1963, Ford was racing in the Indianapolis 500 with Lotus, and Jim Clark took a debut second place with a 255cu.in. (4.2 litre) V8. This dry-sump engine was based on the 260cu.in. Fairlane V8, sleeved to meet Indy regulations, with aluminium alloy block and heads, and the pushrods replaced by four overhead camshafts.

The holy grail of Le Mans still beckoned, and the question for Dearborn was what to race in the French 24 Hours? Americans had a history at Le Mans, but not yet a win: a Stutz had finished second in 1928; Briggs Cunningham Cadillacs ran to 10th and 11th in 1950; and Chrysler-powered Cunningham C5-Rs were third in both 1953 and 1954.

Ford was by now funding Shelby American Inc to the tune of $3 million. Texan Shelby had won Le Mans for Aston Martin in 1959, but was no longer driving after a congenital heart condition had been diagnosed; he had got together a bunch of LA hot-rodders to prepare and race cars at his Venice, California workshops. He surrounded himself with outstanding talent, in particular project manager Carroll Smith and race engineer Phil Remington.

Shelby had identified the low-volume AC Ace as a suitable platform for Ford's small-block 4.7 (289cu.in.) pushrod V8, and the Cobra was born. As his works and customer cars started to clean up West Coast racing, it made waves with Ford, and they bankrolled him for both the Cobra and Mustang GT350 programmes. By the spring of 1963, Shelby announced that he was seeking FIA homologation for the Cobra in the FIA International GT Championship, and took the cars to Europe to run against the Ferrari 250GTO.

That same spring, Henry 'The Deuce' Ford and his top managers attended the Sebring 12 Hours in the hope of seeing the Cobras sweep the board; what they saw instead was a Ferrari 1-2-3-4-5-6, while the best Cobra, in the hands of Phil Hill and Ken Miles, could not better 11th.

'That's the way to go racing,' Ford is reported to have said. 'Why don't we buy those red cars?'

Ferrari had made Le Mans virtually its own since 1949, when the 166 MM *Barchetta* of Luigi Chinetti and Lord Selsdon won the first post-war 24 Hours. Enzo Ferrari, a former driver himself, already had history at Le Mans, giving Alfa Romeo its four wins between 1931 and 1934 as racing manager, but he broke with Alfa in 1939. He set up a new business in nearby Maranello, where he created his own cars. Ironically, it was bombed by the Americans in November 1944 – quite possibly by Liberators built at Ford's Willow Springs wartime aircraft plant.

Equally ironically, he had been introduced to a successful young American driver in 1955, and was impressed enough to offer him a contract. Carroll Shelby turned him down (when nobody ever turned down *Il Commendatore*) because of the internal politics he had seen during his visits to the factory, and went to Aston Martin instead.

By June 1958, Ferrari had taken his second outright Le Mans 24 Hours win, but with a new face behind the wheel, the team's first American signing, Phil Hill. 'Legions of fans watched the exhausted drivers cruise by, knowing that with an American champion crowned for the first time at Europe's greatest race, American

● After Enzo Ferrari rebuffed Henry Ford II's efforts to buy 90% of his company, things got personal. While *Il Commendatore* (below) rarely attended races, The Deuce was present at every Le Mans his cars contested.
The Revs Institute for Automotive Research/ Eric della Faille

cars couldn't be far behind,' wrote AJ Baime, in *Go Like Hell*.

A few weeks after the 1963 Sebring race, a deputation from Ford, led by Ford Division assistant general manager Don Frey, was on its way to Maranello to discuss a 90 per cent buy-out, with the concession that Enzo Ferrari would still run the racing side. The race cars would be called Ferrari-Fords, the road cars Ford-Ferraris.

But despite weeks of negotiation, and with a price of $15 million mutually agreed, the talks collapsed, and Enzo Ferrari pulled the plug, refusing to accept Ford's veto on where, when and by whom his cars were raced.

'If I wish to enter cars at Indianapolis and you do not wish me to, do we go or do we not go?', asked Ferrari. Frey replied, 'You do not go'. At that point, the talks ended. Ferrari never got over the perceived slight, and eventually went to Gianni Agnelli of Fiat to form an alliance 'to protect Ferrari against any future American takeover bid'.

It would have been an unlikely marriage, had it happened – Fords had rolled off mass-production lines since the early 20th century, whilst Ferraris were jewels, lovingly hand-built by craftsmen whose fathers and grandfathers had learned their trade as blacksmiths and armourers. In 1963, Ferrari was producing 600 cars per year; Ford's River Rouge plant alone was building 1,200 cars per day.

● Ford was already bankrolling Carroll Shelby's Ford Cobra programme, which was cleaning up US racing and now making inroads into European GT. But it needed a car which could take the fight to Ferrari for overall victory at Le Mans.
The Revs Institute for Automotive Research/ Albert Bochroch

● It already had an engine lined up – the 4.2-litre V8 which had powered Jim Clark's Lotus-Ford to a debut second place in the 1963 Indianapolis 500, and which would win in 1965. The overhead camshafts were replaced by pushrods for the endurance programme.
The Revs Institute for Automotive Research/ Karl Ludvigsen

Chapter 2
The Birth of the GT40

After the failed attempt to buy Ferrari, Ford's credo became 'if you can't join them, beat them' and, in July 1963, designer Roy Lunn at Ford's Research & Development department was commissioned to come up with a Le Mans winner.

Briton Lunn was a design genius who had already made a big impact in European racing, when, at the age of 24, he penned the Aston Martin DB2s which took class wins at Le Mans, in 1950 and 1951, before moving first to Jowett, and then to Ford of England. He went to work for the Ford parent company in America in 1958, in the design and engineering studio under Eugene Bordinat.

In April 1963, Englishman John Wyer, the architect of Aston Martin's Le Mans and World Sports Car Championship successes, met Ford executive Ray Geddes whilst visiting his old friend Carroll Shelby in Los Angeles. Geddes was aware that Aston was ending its factory motorsport programme, and Wyer was invited to stop at Dearborn on the way home for further talks with Geddes's boss, Don Frey.

'I had absolutely no thought of employment with Ford Motor Company,' related Wyer in his autobiography *The Certain Sound*. 'I had decided that whatever I did next, it would be as far removed as possible from racing and sports cars.'

Nevertheless, following a visit from Frey, Geddes and Lunn (with whom Wyer had worked at Aston Martin), Wyer found himself accepting an offer to more than double his Aston Martin salary.

He already had in mind a suitable base vehicle for the project: Eric Broadley's Lola Mk6 GT. Mid-engined was now the way to go: Formula 1 cars, starting with Cooper, and soon followed by the rest, had already put the power behind the driver. In 1963, Ferrari's new 250P followed Lola into sports car racing with a mid-mounted V12, a radical departure for Maranello.

Wyer was given a first-year budget of $1.7 million to construct four race cars and to run the race operation, overseen by a new Dearborn-based division, Special Vehicles Activity, under Frank Zimmerman. In July, Lunn joined Wyer in Britain as head of engineering, along with three other Ford engineers: two were Englishmen, chassis designer Len Bailey and body designer Ron Martin, and the third was an American, Chuck Mountain.

Eric Broadley was at this time working out of a small workshop in Bromley, Kent, constructing his mid-engined monocoque GT prototype, which employed the 260cu.in. (4.2 litre) Ford Indy V8. The 35-year old English driver and engineer had already built a series of racing cars, including the mid-engined Mk4 Formula 1 car which took Bowmaker Racing's John Surtees to fourth place in the 1962 world championship. Dearborn asked Wyer to take him on board, and Ford bought two Lola GT prototypes as test mules, the suspension elements of which were modified to simulate the Ford GT.

To start with they worked in Lola's cramped premises, sharing staff and even Lola's bank account. After initial tests to check new parts, the two Lolas were taken to Monza, one with new Ford suspension, to get back-to-back comparisons between Ford and Lola thinking.

'But the second, original, Lola never turned a wheel,

Unveiled at the 1964 Detroit Auto Show, the Ford GT – as it was originally titled – was a sensation, and even John Wyer, pictured right with designer Roy Lunn, allowed himself a rare smile. Its 40-inch height (actually, 40.5in.) saw it soon renamed the GT40.
The Revs Institute for Automotive Research/ Karl Ludvigsen

The Birth of the GT40

● The jewel-like 4.2 Indy engine nestles in the back of GT/101, awaiting the exhaust tailpipes, with the Colotti transaxle behind. The four-link independent rear suspension was developed on an IBM 704 computer, which filled an entire room at Ford's Dearborn engineering centre.
The Revs Institute for Automotive Research/George Phillips

denying ourselves any comparison,' said Wyer. 'An endurance test – certainly no less than 1,000 km - with it would have at least given us valuable information about the durability of components, in particular the Colotti transmission. But the Ford engineers were convinced their ideas were better than Broadley's.'

Wyer always strongly made the point that the Ford GT was not a modified version of the Lola GT. 'Nothing could be further from the truth,' he wrote. 'Both cars were mid-engined coupes, using a Ford engine, but any resemblance ended there. The Lola GT was a simple concept which set a trend, and for which Eric Broadley is entitled to great credit, but the GT40 was an original concept, extremely sophisticated and, for its purpose, over-engineered.'

Whilst on a visit in August to Dearborn, Wyer, now 53, was shown the full-size clay mock-up of what was to become the GT40, taking its design cues from the futuristic 1962 Mustang I concept. 'I thought it was the most beautiful and functional car I had ever seen,' he recalled.

The mock-up was white and blue, US racing colours under which Briggs Cunningham had proudly competed at Le Mans in the 1950s. Notably, it was the first racing car to employ computers in its design – this was six years before the first moon-landing - and was also tested in an aircraft wind-tunnel using a 3/8th scale aerodynamic model.

There were now just 250 days to Le Mans 1964; by October, Wyer had found larger premises in Yeovil Road, Slough, close to London's Heathrow Airport, to which Lola also moved. But inevitably, as so often happens among brilliant minds, there was friction between Lunn and Broadley.

The first two cars, GT/101 and GT/102, were built at Slough between September 1963 and March 1964, using Abbey Panels of Coventry for the steel chassis, a monocoque with the roof as an extra stressed member. Glass-fibre body panels were made at Peter and David Jackson's Specialised Mouldings workshop at London's Crystal Palace; the Ford Styling body mock-up had been shipped to them In October.

The independent suspension had been designed at Dearborn by Chuck Carring, using a room-sized IBM 1704 computer. Armstrong dampers were fitted, but planned Halibrand magnesium wheels were replaced by 15in. spoked Borranis to aid the cooling of the cast-iron Girling brake discs, and shod with Dunlop racing tyres.

The 4.2 litre engine was based on Ford's Indianapolis all-aluminium dry-sump V8 but with pushrods rather than OHC, and four Weber carburettors in place of the Hilborn fuel injection. It delivered 350bhp at 7,000rpm, with 275lb/ft of torque at 5,600rpm.

The transmission was as used by the Lotus Indycar and the Lola GT - a Colotti transaxle (coincidentally built in Ferrari's home town of Modena), with Metalastic driveshaft couplings. Two rubber fuel bladders, wrapped in fireproof neoprene – one beneath each door sill – provided the maximum 42 gallons permitted by Le Mans regulations. Space was provided for the mandatory spare wheel in the nose, and the two luggage boxes demanded by outdated FIA regulations, in the rear. It also had a much-vaunted airflow system through the cabin, including ventilation holes in the seats, but that never worked as intended.

The prototype Ford GT was right-hand-drive with a right-hand gear change, as would be all the Ford prototypes which followed; with the majority of circuits clockwise, the driver was better-located for predominantly right-hand corners and to see pit-signals in those pre-radio days.

The car's development was not without drama – there was huge pressure from Dearborn to race at Sebring in March 1964, but Wyer made it absolutely clear that he could not meet this deadline. Iacocca acceded, and instead insisted that 'The World Car: American engine, Italian transmission and English brakes', should be launched at a New York Auto Show press conference on 3 April 1964, 11 months after it was first conceived.

Wyer again protested, 'but quite in vain, and I believe that this was one of the more fateful decisions in the GT40 saga, because of the time which was to be wasted in preparing the first car as a show model, and not testing it prior to Le Mans. The GT40's parent and paymaster was a Ford marketing division, our small team was working in a glare of publicity, and we were constantly under pressure to make optimistic forecasts for which there was no sound engineering validity.'

The launch of what was then still named simply Ford GT was, however, an unqualified success. The media fell over itself in praise for the beautiful, low race car, hailed as the future of sports car racing, and even the normally dour Wyer (who had given British press a sneak preview at Heathrow) allowed himself some satisfaction at its reception. Iacocca told the press, 'The Ford GT is more than a car, it's a test of Ford engineering and ability. In going into GT racing, we feel we are accepting the toughest challenge presently available to the minds and talents of motor car builders.'

On his return from New York, Wyer met Zimmerman with Ford of Britain's Leonard Crossland and Walter Hayes in London, to set up Ford Advanced Vehicles (FAV) as a subsidiary of Ford of Britain,

financed by Dearborn.

Wyer took on-board his former Aston Martin colleague John Horsman, a Cambridge engineering graduate, as his number 2. 'There was a lot to do', Horsman told *Motor Sport*, 'because the car was unstable. The guys who had originally designed it had no racing experience, so it was too heavy, and the engine was no good.'

Dealing with a major corporation was the hardest part of the job, Horsman recalled. 'We had a very hard time. John would go to the States and have a meeting with the powers that be, but there were too many fingers in the pot and not much got done. They would eventually take decisions, but by the time John returned to base it had all changed, so his trip served no purpose. It was a case of order, counter-order, and disorder!'

● Eric Broadley's pretty little 1963 Lola GT was not the only mid-engined sports car – a Ferrari 250P had already won Le Mans with the power behind the driver – but its glass-fibre body, monocoque chassis and Ford V8 heralded a new dawn.
Ferret Fotographics

The Birth of the GT40

Wyer's earlier pessimism was well-founded, as after a hurried Goodwood test on his return home, the wet Le Mans Test Weekend at the end of April was an unmitigated disaster. The prototype had run for only four hours, and none of those at full power. Drivers Roy Salvadori and Jo Schlesser (subbing for Bruce McLaren, who was racing at Aintree) reported that the cars were dangerously unstable above 170mph, at which speed they were getting wheelspin. Yet they were geared for 200mph on the 3.7-mile Mulsanne Straight.

Wyer suggested it was an aerodynamic problem which could be cured by spoilers, as he had found at Aston Martin, and Broadley backed him; Lunn disagreed, insisting that it was a suspension geometry problem, and adjustments were made accordingly. Salvadori refused to continue when a door flew off, but Schlesser persevered, only to take off at the Mulsanne kink, destroying GT/101 and fortunate to walk away little more than shaken. Salvadori was persuaded to drive again the next day, but he too crashed. On returning to the UK, he asked to be released from his

- The GT40s first track appearance ended in disaster at the April 1964 Le Mans tests – Jo Schlesser left a 100-metre debris trail as he wrote off GT/101. Roy Salvadori too had problems with the aerodynamically-unstable design, and walked away from the project.
Ford

- Hurried tests at MIRA gave the car a rear spoiler which transformed the handling. Bruce McLaren and Phil Hill debuted GT/102 in the Nürburgring 1000 Kms, but had transmission problems before a suspension breakage ended its race.
Ford

contract, to which Wyer reluctantly agreed.

So, just six weeks before the 1964 Le Mans 24 Hours, Wyer had one car wrecked and the other (GT/102) damaged, with only one confirmed driver – Schlesser - for a three-car entry. Two more chassis (GT/103 and GT/104) were hurriedly completed. American Phil Hill and New Zealander Bruce McLaren, Americans Richie Ginther and Masten Gregory, and Briton Richard Attwood were quickly signed up, the latter to join Schlesser.

Back in Britain, testing at the banked MIRA track, it was found that a 4.5-inch rear spoiler transformed the cars' handling – 'hands off at 170mph', reported McLaren - and this was to be a trademark of all Ford GTs from then on. Prior to that, Lunn had likened the car's tapering aerodynamics to 'an arrow without feathers'.

But before the French race came the Nürburgring 1,000Km, at which a singleton Ford – the repaired Salvadori Le Mans Test car - made the Ford GT's competition debut in the hands of Phil Hill, Ferrari's 1961 F1 world champion, and Bruce McLaren. After

Two new cars joined GT/102 for Le Mans 1964: 102 goes through Le Pesage – scrutineering – ahead of the 103 of Ginther and Gregory. Both went out with transmission failures, while the 104 of Attwood/Schlesser caught fire at Mulsanne corner.
Ford

After losing 22 minutes with a blocked carburettor jet in the first hour, 102 (no.10) climbed back to fourth place in the hands of Hill and McLaren. McLaren set a new lap record before the clutch failed and Ford's first Le Mans was over.
Ford

The Birth of the GT40

- The Fords were still being prepared during Le Mans qualifying – GT/102 has yet to have nose tabs fitted to keep the front end from lifting (compare with the race photo on the previous page). Wyer said the development programme was too rushed and too public.
Ford

qualifying second to the John Surtees/Lorenzo Bandini Ferrari 275P, it stayed with the leaders for 11 laps of the 22.8km (14.2 mile) *Nordschleife*, before a rear suspension mounting point broke, ending its race. However, the transmission had been protesting throughout, frequently jumping out of gear.

Le Mans was just three weeks later, far too short a timescale after the rigours of the 'Ring. But FAV rose to the occasion, and fielded the three GTs with improved high-speed stability, which qualified second, fourth, and ninth in the 57-car field.

The race started well enough, with Ginther passing three Ferraris for the lead at over 200mph on the Mulsanne straight but Hill lost 22 minutes in the first hour in five pit-stops with a blocked carburettor jet. The Ginther/Gregory car retired after four hours stuck in second gear and Attwood's GT/104 was gutted by fire when a nylon fuel pipe melted from the exhaust heat.

Meanwhile, the Hill/McLaren car was having an extraordinary run, climbing from 23rd to sixth by midnight. McLaren then moved it up to fourth, recalling, 'my four-hour stint from midnight into Sunday morning was the best 500 miles I ever covered'. But it was all over by 5.20am, when the clutch failed, although he had set a new lap record shortly before retirement.

It was not lost on Dearborn - embarrassingly for Slough - that the Shelby Cobra Daytona Coupe of Americans Dan Gurney and Bob Bondurant had finished fourth overall, behind three Ferrari prototypes, to win the GT category.

Frank Zimmerman had by now been promoted within Ford, and was replaced as head of SVA by 46-year old Brussels-based Leo Beebe, who had survived the disastrous Edsel road car launch and was seen as The Deuce's troubleshooter in Europe. His brief from Iacocca, he recalled, 'was to win Daytona, Indy and Le Mans - one hell of a challenge'.

Beebe had been at Le Mans watching the debacle unfold, and on the Monday morning called a meeting at the Hotel de Paris at Le Mans to discuss what had gone wrong.

He and Wyer were immediately at loggerheads – Wyer wanted to replace the fragile Colotti transmission with the sturdier German Zahnradfabrik (ZF) transaxle. But Beebe insisted that they race three cars in the Reims 12 Hours three weeks later, with a new car, GT/105, fitted with the 4.7 litre Cobra V8, to replace Attwood's fire-damaged GT/104.

Almost predictably, two of the cars went out with gearbox failure, the transmissions again unable to cope with the massive grunt of the V8s and the multiple gearshifts. The third GT, that of Hill and McLaren, retired with a broken crankshaft, 'which no doubt saved us from a transmission grand slam', wryly noted Wyer, who now had just three all-alloy V8s left.

He took the decision to change all the cars to the iron-block, wet-sump Cobra V8, which as well as giving a power (370bhp) and torque boost, could be machined out to 5.0 litres or more if required, and was also lighter without the dry-sump equipment of the 4.2 V8. He also ordered ZF transmissions, although delivery would not begin until March at the earliest. By then Wyer had the green light to start the production run of 100 cars.

The deteriorating relationship between Lunn and Broadley had by now reached crisis point. Larger, more suitable premises in Slough's Banbury Avenue had already been located for production of what was now named the GT40, and as Lunn was Ford's man, it would not be him who was leaving. So Broadley was handsomely paid off in June, and was left to concentrate on his own Lola Cars business in Yeovil Road, eventually to produce the legendary Lola T70 sports car.

Ford had contested three races with seven cars,

The Birth of the GT40

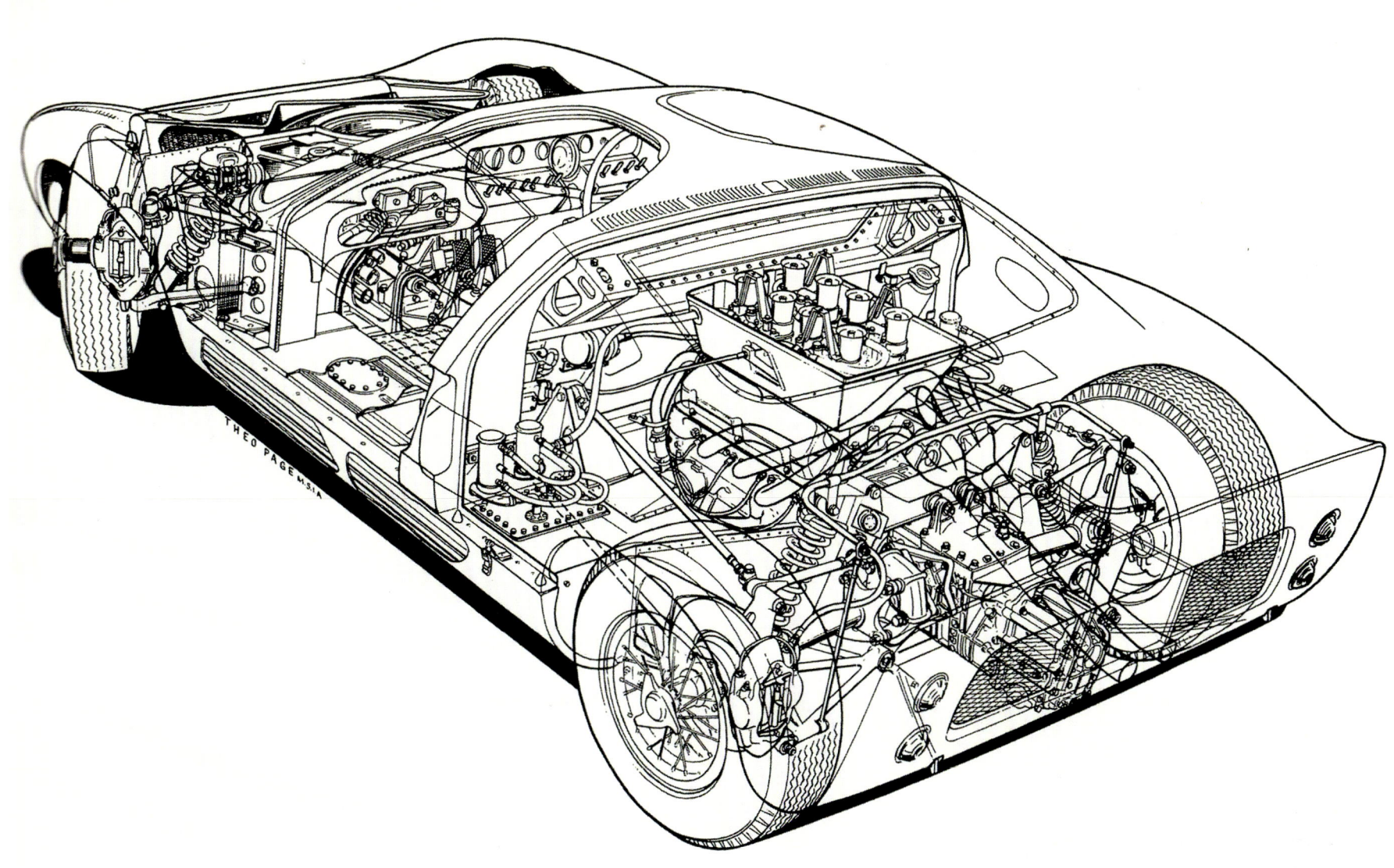

and had yet to post a finish. Because of the repeated failures, Don Frey cancelled plans to race the cars in the US that autumn, and instead FAV concentrated on intensive testing in Europe throughout the final three months of 1964. Progress was slow, not helped when GT/102 was destroyed at Monza after Sir John Whitmore had the throttle stick open; the car ended up in the trees, but the racing baronet was thankfully unhurt.

The final indignity of 1964 was at the non-championship Nassau Speed Week in December, where Ford insisted a reluctant Wyer should field two cars. Both failed to finish: Hill (head gasket) and McLaren (front suspension), topping off a disastrous debut season.

'I regarded Nassau as a serious distraction from our development programme', recalled Wyer. 'Because I lost the argument, I was thoroughly bloody-minded, and took no interest in the preparation. It was a stupid attitude, and it gave our critics another weapon to use against us, and they were quick to make use of it.'

Technical artist Theo Page's cutaway drawing of the first Ford GT shows the monocoque chassis, front and rear suspensions, Ford V8 and Colotti transmission in X-ray detail.

The Birth of the GT40

John Wyer

The son of a Sunbeam dealer, as a schoolboy, John Wyer's interest in motorsport was kindled by the company's successes at Brooklands, so it was natural that in 1927 he would join Sunbeam as an apprentice engineer. In 1932 he went to Solex Carburettors where he was to work until the end of World War II. During this time he bought a Bugatti to rebuild as a race car. He was later to swap it for an HRG, with which he competed in hill-climbs, and then moved on to work on Aston Martins for a friend's racing team.

In 1950, Aston Martin appointed him its team manager, and so started his long affair with Le Mans, through DB2, DB3 and on to DBR1, which won the 1959 24 Hours driven by Roy Salvadori and Carroll Shelby. With wins also at the Nürburgring and in the Goodwood TT, Aston Martin claimed the 1959 sports car world championship.

Wyer – known by his workers as 'Death Ray', with a stare that could kill - stayed with Aston Martin until 1963, overseeing the development of the DB4 and with further racing successes. But he had his differences with Aston's owner David Brown which decided him to look for pastures new when, coincidentally, in America for the New York Auto Show and a tour of US Aston Martin dealers, he paid a visit to Carroll Shelby in Los Angeles.

Ford's Ray Geddes happened to be checking on Ford's hefty investment in Shelby American that same afternoon, and the outcome of that chance meeting was that Wyer was to be given the job of building and running the Ford GT40 to beat Ferrari

● A taciturn John Wyer surveys his domain, the Ford pits at Le Mans; in 1959 he oversaw Aston Martin's victory in the 24 Hours, Carroll Shelby bringing in DBR1 with Roy Salvadori behind him. Both joined him on his Ford GT40 adventure.
LAT Images

at Le Mans, and was to set up Ford Advanced Vehicles in England. His early recruits included John Horsman, an engineer from Aston Martin and designers Eric Broadley and Len Bailey.

'Lots of people denigrated John, but he was brilliant in every way', Horsman later told *Motor Sport*. 'He'd think very hard – and didn't sleep very much as a result – but that meant he could come up with a valid reason to do something one way, then think hard again and come up with an equally valid reason to do it another! His final decisions were usually right, though. He had a reputation for rudeness, but I think he was just quite shy.'

While the first year, 1964, was to prove disappointing, it was not through want of Wyer's efforts to get corporate America to understand that racing teams could not be run by suits and accountants. He was frequently thwarted, particularly over the choice of the right transmission, and for 1965 Dearborn took the race programme from him and handed it to Shelby, although he was still to build the GT40 for the factory and customers, and develop the Mk III road car version.

Shelby fared little better in his first season but it all came together for Ford in 1966 with a Le Mans 1-2-3 for the Slough-sourced Mk II, and repeated the win in 1967 with the American-built Mk IV. Wyer had not been idle during this time, still running customer cars in the world championship and at Le Mans, and his moment was still to come.

Job done, Ford ended its own GT programme, and paid off Wyer, but contracted him to continue with the GT40 build – now close to 100 cars. He closed down FAV, and set up JW Automotive Engineering with his friend John Willment, with Horsman as executive director and David Yorke as team manager. It was funded by Gulf Oil through American Grady Davis. Part of the funding was used to develop the Mirage, a slimline version of the GT40, but JW still had confidence in the GT40. Incorporating everything that he had wanted to do two years earlier, he took victory at Le Mans in 1968 and 1969, giving Ford a four-year winning streak.

Then came the Porsche years, JWAE Gulf 917s taking 11 wins (and a 12th with the 908-3 in the Targa Florio) to claim the world sports car championship in both 1970 and 1971, but never the Le Mans 24 Hours – that happened only in the Steve McQueen film! In October 1971 Porsche announced – without a word to JWAE or to Gulf – that it was handing its race operation to Roger Penske in the United States. 'We had won 12 races for Porsche and, of course, the World Championship for Makes in both years', wrote Wyer in his biography. 'I did not expect to be given the Knight's Cross with Oak Leaves, but thought we might deserve a telegram or letter. In fact, we received neither.'

Although by now semi-retired, Wyer had to wait until 1975 for his fourth and final Le Mans win, with the Ford DFV–powered Gulf Mirage run by Horsman and designed by Bailey, in the hands of Jacky Ickx and Derek Bell. In 1976 the team was sold to American Harley Cluxton III. Wyer died in Scottsdale, Arizona in 1989, aged 79.

Wyer would win the Le Mans 24 Hours four times in all, but not with the fearsome Gulf Porsches, despite taking the 917s to two world titles; here at Brands Hatch Pedro Rodriguez does what he loved best, winning in the rain.
LAT Images

Chapter 3
Shelby takes control

The omnipresent Leo Beebe had been in Nassau and seen the failure of the two Fords in the last race of the year. After a short, terse team debriefing, he removed the factory race programme from FAV, and handed it to Shelby American.

Beebe ordered the two Nassau cars to be delivered to Shelby's Venice workshop. It would not be until March 1965 that Shelby was to move to more spacious premises – a former P51 Mustang fighter factory at Los Angeles International Airport - where the GT40/Daytona Coupe race shop and hand-assembly line for Cobras and Shelby GT350s (which would eventually roll out at 125 per month) were in neighbouring hangars.

So in mid-December, chassis GT/103 and GT/104 arrived by TWA Freight, and a new chapter in the Ford GT story began – but not before the two travel-stained and race-weary cars had been thoroughly steam-cleaned, stripped and rebuilt, then repainted in Shelby's own dark blue colours.

Shelby's Cobra development driver, World War 2 tank driver Englishman Ken Miles, took GT/103 to Riverside and Willow Springs racetracks to try it out. His initial impression was not good; 'the car is bloody awful', he reported after the first run.

Work started on improving the car: the iron-block Shelby 4.7 V8 was tuned up; a Ford aerospace contractor fitted computers in the passenger seat to measure engine, brake and suspension performance; and cotton yarns were taped to the bodywork and photographed to check aerodynamic flow.

Wider Halibrand magnesium wheels replaced the spoked Borannis, saving 14kg of unsprung weight, with wider Goodyear tyres, and larger front brakes, using Kelsey-Hayes ventilated discs all round. With ZF transmissions ruled out because of the delivery delay, Shelby stripped the Colotti casing of its Italian gears, and inserted Ford helical gears with an uprated differential.

Other work overseen by Phil Remington – whom Dan Gurney described as 'a fireman looking for a fire, he was so quick coming up with solutions' - included relocating the engine and gearbox oil coolers to the rear of the car either side of the transaxle, which opened up room for a larger front water radiator. Intake ducts were enlarged to improve cooling to the brakes.

In January 1965, Ford revealed its competition plans to the media at Riverside circuit in California. Beebe and Geddes formally announced that the Ford GT racing programme had been transferred to Shelby American Inc, which would enter the factory cars at Daytona, Sebring and Le Mans, while John Wyer (who was present at Riverside) would continue to run FAV out of Slough, building the 100 production cars for Ford or for sale (at £6,500, including tax), and support private customers in international racing. FAV was also to enter a factory car in selected races, including Le Mans, until there were sufficient privateer entries.

The first race for the Shelby GT40s was the 1965 Daytona Continental 2,000Km, the first time Ford had been up against Ferrari's new 410bhp 330P2. The Italian factory was absent, despite the race's world championship status, so the car was entered by US Ferrari importer Luigi Chinetti's NART team for works drivers John Surtees and Pedro Rodriguez.

Under new management. Carroll Shelby (right) and his talented English development driver Ken Miles, who learned his trade as a World War 2 tank driver. By 1966, they had helped to turn the original GT40 into the winning 7-litre Mk II. *The Revs Institute for Automotive Research/Eric della Faille*

Shelby takes control

- Miles, Shelby and Lloyd Ruby celebrate the GT40's first win, the 1965 Daytona Continental, in GT/103, now run by Shelby American with the 4.7-litre V8 from the Cobra. It also was the first race finish for any Ford GT40.
Claude Nahum collection/ Gerard Crombac

- GT/103 on its way to that all-important first victory at Daytona International Speedway. The Continental was a 2,000 Km race lasting just over 12 hours, showing not only speed but reliability. It was the first of six wins for Shelby-run Ford GT40 derivatives.
Getty Images/RacingOne

The Ferrari took pole as the GT40s struggled with handling on the Florida banking; this was cured by driver Richie Ginther's suggestion of mini-spoilers either side of the air intake, which reduced both understeer and lift. The Kelsey-Hayes ventilated brake discs started cracking and were quickly replaced by the original, solid Girlings.

Ford won, Ken Miles and Lloyd Ruby in GT/103 marking not only the GT40's first victory, but the first race in which any GT40 had finished. GT/104 in the hands of Ginther and Bob Bondurant was third after losing 27 minutes changing the starter motor, while the Ferrari broke its transmission. The tide had finally turned.

Next came the Sebring 12 Hours, still in Florida, where Chaparral had been encouraged to enter by race promoter Alex Ulman, although it would be ineligible for manufacturer's points. The Chevrolet-powered 2C took the chequered flag first, after the race had been all but washed out by massive rain and flooding – spare wheels were seen floating down the pit lane - but the Ford of McLaren and Miles (again GT/103) was given the points win. It may have been a hollow victory for publicity purposes, but it was still a second successive win in world championship race: Daytona, Sebring - now Le Mans could be the Triple Crown.

Ford had been pushing for a 'lightweight' version of the Holman & Moody 427cu.in (7-litre) Galaxie NASCAR engine, against Wyer's continual advice on weight grounds, which would be detrimental to both brakes and transmission, and which in any case, he considered was not necessary as performance had never been an issue. The big-block dry-sump V8 would weigh 66kg more than the 4.7 V8, even with alloy heads in place of the NASCAR iron, and would take the car's overall weight to 1,360kg. But Beebe prevailed, and ordered a 7-litre GT40 to be built for 1966. It was codenamed X but soon to be titled the Mk II. Roy Lunn went back

to Dearborn to work on the re-design.

Enter Kar Kraft, Nick Hartmann's Ford racing company, which had been taken in-house at Dearborn under Lunn's wing. The first two cars delivered to Kar Kraft from FAV were GT/106 and GT/107, where Hartmann, Lunn and their teams modified the chassis, adopting lessons learned at Daytona, then shoehorned in the 425bhp 7 litre engines built at Dearborn by Ford Engine & Foundry.

A single Holley 4-barrel carburettor and a massive snake-pit exhaust system were the trademarks of the 427, for which further changes had to be made to the car, and the man who would be sent to Charlotte and Los Angeles to check out the installation and settings, was E&F engine specialist Mose Nowland.

Money was no object. 'We could do anything we wanted', remembers Nowland. 'If it was a sensible choice, and there was a need for it to help speed or durability or performance, we had no problem getting it.

'It was already obvious we were going to have to retire the little engine and go with the big 427. Even with modifications to fix the weakness of the 289, it just didn't get the job done.'

Nowland was just 26 years old when the project got underway: 'I was a very fortunate young man, they were wonderful times and I was lucky to be working with Ford as we were pushing performance boundaries.'

Dyno running of the 427 at Dearborn saw 40-hour tests, with a robotic gearshifter simulating the gearchanges around the 13km of the Le Mans circuit. 'We saw that, at 6,200rpm, we could run in top gear at 220mph', recalls Lee Holman. 'The engine was understated and under-tuned, which meant reliability.'

The rear bulkhead and seats were moved forward to allow for the extra length of the engine – not a major problem, as the GT40 had started life with a moveable pedal box, rather than adjustable seats - and the water pump was relocated in a bulge between the seats. The

● Ford's omnipresent troubleshooter Leo Beebe may not have been popular in the pits, but he was a mover and shaker who got results; the programme moved up several notches once the American took control.
The Revs Institute for Automotive Research/Albert Bochroch

● The 'snakepit' is how crewmen referred to the engine bays of the two 7-litre powered Mk IIs which Shelby ran at Le Mans in 1965. Note the 4-barrel Holley carburettor, and Ford T-44 transaxle; both cars went out with transmission failure.
The Revs Institute for Automotive Research/Eric della Faille

Shelby takes control

● Ford's entry for the 1965 race included four 4.7-litre GT40s for Rob Walker (foreground), FAV, George Fillipinetti and Ford France, the last a roadster. None finished, leading to an angry exchange between Walker and Henry Ford II. *The Revs Institute for Automotive Research/Eric della Faille*

front end also had to be lengthened to hold the wider spare wheel.

The Achilles' heel of the whole programme to date had been the transmission, and rather than go down the Shelby route, Kar Kraft went for a modified version of Ford's four-speed manual 'Toploader', already found in 427-powered muscle cars like the Mustang.

Transmission expert Ed Hill and his team came up with a magnesium transaxle case to hold it, with a Hewland-like rear cover for quick ratio changes. It was designated the T-44. Because the gears and pinions had to be run-in, Kar Kraft was persuaded to do this on the dyno before delivery, rather than Shelby having to use up precious track time

Initial testing of GT/106 at Ford's Dearborn test track in May 1965 – just five weeks before Le Mans - was positive, with Ford dealer and weekend racer Tom Payne putting in the Mk II's first miles. Then, a week later, he and Ken Miles ran the car at Ford's Romeo, Michigan, high-speed 5-mile track, where Miles saw 210mph. The decision was taken there and then to enter two MK IIs at Le Mans, although the April test weekend had already been and gone, and GT/107 had yet to turn a wheel.

The Blue Oval's optimism received a boost when Jim Clark's 'Powered by Ford' Lotus 38 won the 1965 Indy

Shelby takes control

500 at a record 150mph pace, just two weeks before the 24 Hours. Perhaps the gods were now smiling.

Ford's entry for the 1965 Le Mans 24 Hours totalled six cars – the two 7-litre Mk IIs for Shelby American (in the hands of Phil Hill/Chris Amon, and Bruce McLaren/Ken Miles); and GT40 Mk Is for FAV (fitted with a shortened, low-drag Len Bailey nose), Ford France (an open-topped roadster), Rob Walker, and Georges Filipinetti. Walker and Filipinetti had originally entered other cars, but at Ford's instigation were requested by Wyer to change to GT40s run by Shelby – a move both would regret.

While the two 7-litre cars were fast in qualifying – which had been cancelled on Wednesday by tree-toppling storms, but replaced with Friday running - they were also inherently unstable down the Mulsanne chute. The Shelby crew added air dams to the long noses, and spoilers and shark fins to the rear deck. Then, after two more fins were added above the front wheels, Phil Hill went out and planted his car on pole, 5.1 seconds faster than John Surtees' Ferrari 330P2.

But in the race, after leading for two hours, both Mk IIs hit problems; Miles was out at 8pm, succumbing to gearbox issues, and Hill retired at 11pm with clutch failure. The Mark I GT40s had all been overheating, the Ford France car suffered a ZF transmission breakage after just 11 laps, and the Walker and Filipinetti cars were out with head gasket failures before the second hour. The FAV entry suffered the same fate at five hours and all six Fords had retired by midnight.

This embarrassing failure was reported to have cost $6 million. To rub salt in the wounds, Ferrari's sixth successive win at Le Mans had been taken not by a factory car, but by New York Ferrari distributor Luigi Chinetti's 250LM with American Masten Gregory and Jochen Rindt on board. To Ford's chagrin, this was the first victory for an American entrant.

Rob Walker, the debonair Formula 1 entrant and heir to a whisky company, was furious at the failure, and wrote a vitriolic letter to Henry Ford, complaining that Ford had failed to honour his tyre choice (Dunlop) and driver choice (Jo Bonnier) by substituting Goodyear and Umberto Maglioli. He finished his missive, 'I am very disappointed that Ford Motor Company should make themselves a laughing stock in European motor racing circles, which they undoubtedly did. I would suggest that the mistake which they made was to employ the most experienced racing manager in the world in John Wyer, and not put him in charge. Although Carroll Shelby is obviously a very competent driver, his experience in organising and managing a team can in no way be compared to that of Mr Wyer…'

Even so, the writing was on the wall; after nine successes (backed by nine world championships), 1965 was to be Ferrari's last outright Le Mans 24 Hours victory, and even they could see the Ford juggernaut rolling ever-closer.

In an effort to improve high-speed stability, Shelby fitted dorsal fins to the rear decks of the two Mk IIs, handcut from aluminium by fabricator Bill Eaton. 'They worked quite well - better than the new Ford gearboxes', he said.
Ford

Chapter 4
Heading to victory

In 1966 there was a sea-change for the GT40 in competition – the FIA mandated the new Appendix J to the International Sporting Code, creating a world championship for Group 4 production sports cars of up to 5 litres. The Ford GT40, with its 4.7-litre V8, was immediately eligible, as production of only 50 cars was required, and FAV had already exceeded that. The 7-litre cars, meantime, could continue to fight for overall honours at Le Mans, and for a new Group 6 prototype championship.

Ford had formed a Le Mans Committee in August 1965 to learn lessons from its Le Mans failures, bringing in department heads from across the Ford empire; Leo Beebe gave control of the Le Mans programme to Jacque Passino and John Cowley, with representatives from Shelby, FAV, and a newcomer, Alan Mann Racing. The committee met regularly for the next 11 months. 'We had realized that it didn't matter how fast you went if you didn't finish', said Beebe, 'That mistake won't be repeated.'

Passino noted that while Shelby had been struggling with the Mk II, Ford's NASCAR campaign with Holman & Moody had been all-conquering, and he was about to throw a spanner in the works for Carroll Shelby.

Holman & Moody was brought into the Mk II programme along with Alan Mann, for a three-pronged attack on the 1966 Le Mans 24 Hours. Ford vice-president Homer Perry was given the job of holding the triumvirate together, and dealing with the respective team managers: Al Dowd for Shelby American, John Wanderer for Holman & Moody, and Alan Mann himself.

The 427 engine was beefed up with cross-bolted main bearing caps, the 273kg NASCAR engine's iron heads, an aluminium water pump and front cover, and a lightened flywheel. A magnesium pan for the dry-sump oil system saved more weight - in all, 23kg - and power was pushed up to 449bhp at 5,800rpm.

The T-44 gearbox was further strengthened, the stock Galaxie gears replaced by purpose-built gears and final drive. Whilst doing this, Kar Kraft experimented with two different automatic transmissions, both with production torque converters as used in the six-cylinder Ford Falcon. One was a 'power-shift' gearbox actuated by hydraulic valves, the other a 'crash' gearbox similar to that used by Chaparral with constant-mesh synchro gears and dog clutches.

Extensive testing by Shelby using the two 1965 Le Mans Mk IIs got underway at Riverside and Daytona, but one of four lightweight chassis ordered started to break apart on the Daytona banking, and was no faster than the GT40 tested there 18 months earlier. In December an engine failed at Daytona.

'The 427 engine is not presently considered reliable enough for either 12-hour or 24-hour races', wrote Dowd in a downbeat post-test memo to Homer Perry. 'The T-44 transaxle is considered to be of dubious reliability for 24-hour races, and the brakes are not presently suitable for 12- or 24-hour races. Shelby American is still of the opinion that the 289 CID engine offers at least equal chances of racing success.'

But however much John Wyer might have felt his warnings had been justified, the die was cast, and with the Daytona 24 Hours only weeks away, Ford was going racing with the 427, which, with further tuning, was

In the Mk II's office: about to fire up the V8, the driver is faced with dials reading rpm, water, oil temperature and pressure, and fuel. To his left the fuse panel, to his right the four-speed gearshift with reverse block. All GT40s were right-shift, right-hand drive.
The Revs Institute for Automotive Research/Eric della Faille

Heading to victory

● The business end of the Mk II, the exhaust pipes exiting either side of the T-44 gearbox. This was the view which the Ferraris had once the Mk II and its Mk IIB derivatives had been perfected.
Claude Nahum collection

The first J-car with its distinctive ● lobster-claw front end debuted at the April 1966 Le Mans tests, and was 1.6s faster than the Mk IIs. Ford decided to continue its development away from competition, and rely on the Mk IIs for its third attempt on the 24 Hours.
The Revs Institute for Automotive Research/Jean Charles Martha

producing 463bhp. After the lightweight chassis failure, heavier gauge sheet-steel monocoques were ordered from Abbey Panels, and suspension pick-up points reinforced, with Koni shock-absorbers replacing the previous Armstrongs. Air ducts were also enlarged to help cool the interior.

With the heavier engine, brakes had continued to be problematic, and from now on ventilated discs were fitted to all cars. Shelby also devised brake discs which could be replaced as quickly as pads; and over at Holman & Moody, Wanderer had come up with spring-loaded brake pads.

During 1965, Wyer had pushed Dearborn to accept the new Len Bailey front end, first raced on the FAV entry at Le Mans, which was found to reduce the car's drag coefficient. 'Dearborn was slow to recognize the value of anything we did,' complained Wyer, 'but we had kept Shelby informed, and passed on any results which seemed interesting.'

It was only in January 1966, that the Americans saw the value of Bailey's shorter nose; when tried on the Mk II test car, it was immediately quicker by 8mph (touching 204mph) around Ford's Kingman, Arizona, 5-mile test track. The test car was P/1016, the subject of this book.

The new nose was fitted to all Mk IIs and GT40s from then on. The Mk II was further improved and refined during an eight-day test in late January at Sebring. 1016 was then delivered to Holman & Moody in Charlotte, where it was fitted with a T-43 'jump box' hydraulic auto transmission. Ford had watched Chaparral's success with its automatic box, and wanted to test the water.

The second Holman & Moody Mk II (P/1031) was delivered only at the start of the Daytona 24 Hours week. Wanderer: 'I saw a lot of things wrong with the car – at 3,000lb it was too goddamned heavy, and the Shelby people had no experience on the high bank, they didn't know how to run Daytona'. He ordered a change to heavier shock-absorbers and springs, and fitted adjustable roll-bars to both his charges.

Meanwhile, at Kar Kraft in Dearborn they were already thinking about what might replace the Mk II. The result was J-car – a narrower version of the Ford GT with a honeycomb monocoque chassis. It would be not only lighter, but sleeker, while retaining the same drivetrain and wheelbase as its predecessor. It was to appear for the first time at the Le Mans Test Weekend in April.

Once again, aerodynamic instability would hamper the J-car's early development, and Shelby's British test driver Ken Miles was to lose his life at Riverside whilst trying to improve it. But after Shelby engineering genius Phil Remington and his team went to work on the body at Ford Styling at Dearborn, it came out with less drag and more speed. The revised car was named the Mk IV - but that was a year ahead. For now, the emphasis was on the first race of the 1966 season at Daytona.

Exceptional Cars

Heading to victory

Ford GT40 MkII 1016

Part 2
The Story of 1016

There was a moment during Ford's four-year factory programme at which everything so far learned gelled, and the Blue Oval realised it now had a winning car on its hands.

That eureka moment came at Sebring in January 1966, during a week-long test of what was to become the Ford Mk II. The workhorse for the test was Ford GT40 P/1016, built at Slough by FAV, but finished in Los Angeles by Shelby American.

Shelby shoehorned in Ford's 7-litre V8, and pounded it around the Florida airfield circuit for seven days, working through a long list of upgrades and updates. By the end of the test, 1016 provided enough feedback to allow Mk IIs to win both the 1966 Daytona 24 Hours and Le Mans 24 Hours with 1-2-3 finishes.

1016 had played a significant role in giving Ford those wins, and indeed was the third-placed car at Le Mans. It was raced only four times, but again helped Ford with its 1967 Le Mans victory by gathering valuable data at the April tests.

Today, resplendent in its show-stopping gold and pink 1966 livery, 1016 continues to appear at historic races, in concours events and at motor shows, revelling in its fame as one of the most important GT40s ever to be produced.

🟡 1016 had its moment of glory at Le Mans 1966, finishing third behind the No.1 and No.2 sister cars. The most distinctive-liveried of the 1966 Mk IIs, it had already played its part in developing the 7-litre model.
LAT Images

Chapter 5
Preparing for battle

GT40 P/1016 was a production car ordered from FAV at Slough on 18 June 1965, and was ready for delivery to Shelby American Inc by 11 August. It was unpainted and untrimmed, had no engine or transmission, no front structure, and no front bodywork.

All FAV GT40s which were intended to become Mk IIs were delivered to Shelby. The conversion work was carried out at his premises alongside Los Angeles International Airport, assisted by the crews from the final recipients: SAI themselves, Holman & Moody, or Alan Mann Racing. They fitted wider, lighter Halibrand wheels with Goodyear or Firestone tyres, lighter glass-fibre bodywork, relocated air ducting to reduce lift and drag, and also modified the rear bodywork with a 4.5in. lip supplied by FAV. The Len Bailey-designed short nose was now fitted to all Mk IIs, as well as to the FAV GT40s.

Thereafter, 1016 was slated for delivery to Holman & Moody, but Ford requisitioned it to run as a test car for the upcoming Daytona 24 Hours. It was completed two weeks early, fitted with a large-block 7-litre Ford V8 (AX-316-1-18) with T-44 four-speed manual transmission (KKL-105). The 427cu.in. engines, built by Ford's Engine and Foundry Division at Dearborn, were now producing 463bhp with alloy heads and other weight-saving parts. Quick-change brake discs were also fitted.

Shelby took 1016, with white and matt-black bodywork (borrowed from P/1011, as its own was not yet ready), to Ford's high-speed test facility at Kingman, Arizona, with Ken Miles at the wheel.

'Finally, the Mk II was getting the development work it had always needed,' wrote AJ Baime in *Go Like Hell*. 'The engine and gearbox were gaining durability, while the Shelby American team was homing in on the most critical issue: the big 427 was so powerful and so heavy, decelerating into corners was proving troublesome, and the half-inch thick cast-iron discs were shattering.'

Then it was on to Sebring for an eight-day test starting on 16 January 1966, where Miles was joined by Holman & Moody's Ronnie Bucknum. That first day, the team worked through a long list of jobs and modifications, which included a swap to transaxle KKL-107, which had a larger pinion bearing. Ford's report of the tests shows that on the first day, 11 laps (57.2 miles) were run during 44 minutes.

On Day 2, after instrumentation had been installed, one of the drivers (which, was not revealed) applied the cold brakes too hard, and the car went off the track backwards, demolishing a cyclone fence. The damage was insignificant, although the report blamed 'poor judgement on driver's part'. The brakes continued to give problems through the second day, and a scheduled change from Girling to Kelsey-Hayes ventilated discs did nothing to help, as the brake fluid continued to boil. A total of 33 laps were completed in 1h 34m.

Day 3 saw early clutch problems, but, more seriously, after 52 laps a front disc shattered, destroying the caliper and hub-carrier, and cast-iron discs were put back on the car. Running resumed after repairs, and when rain came after 84 laps the team was able to compare Goodyear dry tyres with Goodyear J wet tyres; both drivers preferred the dry tyres in the damp conditions as the Js would not heat up, nor could they be scrubbed-in. Some 104 laps were run during the day over a six-hour period; fuel mileage

Daytona and Sebring featured in the pre-1966 season test programme as the 4.7 GT40s became 7-litre Mk IIs. Here in the Daytona Shelby garage, the 24 Hour-winning No. 98 car of Miles/Ruby and second-placed No. 97 of Gurney/Grant are prepared.
The Revs Institute for Automotive Research/Karl Ludvigsen

Preparing for battle

Rare shots of 1016 during early 1966 tests, using borrowed bodywork. The front end has been lengthened for the wider mandatory spare wheel. At the rear is the Ford T-34 two-speed automatic transmission, which was used at Daytona but replaced with the T-44 manual for Le Mans.
Claude Nahum collection

in the dry was given as 4.6mpg (US).

It rained most of Day 4, so rather than endurance running, Shelby did rain tyre testing; the Goodyear K was preferred to the J, with better traction, cornering and aquaplaning resistance. 41 laps were covered in 2h 24m.

Orders came from Engine & Foundry at Dearborn to plug the oil-cooler and crankcase breather plugs – 'Shelby American fully agreed with this' read the test notes – but there were clutch problems, finally resolved by changing roll pins with bolts. There was another front brake disc failure, but by now Shelby American cast-iron discs with ventilation grooves and Raybestos pads had arrived, so were fitted. 31 laps were covered in 1h 34m.

Saturday was another wet day. Moderate rain and deep puddles limited running to 35 laps to evaluate Goodyear against Firestone rain tyres; the Goodyear K was again the best, while one type of Firestone was noted as 'terrible under all conditions'.

On the Sunday, the weather had improved, and in the dry, brake durability was tested; disc cooling had been improved by more ducting to direct air on to the brakes, and the new Shelby discs were said to be 'excellent'. The drivers were ordered to punish the brakes to simulate race conditions, and found that braking power had been greatly improved.

The final day of the test was Monday, 23 January, and an initial 10 laps were run at half-throttle to bed in the transaxle. As soon as this was done, a valve spring broke on the first lap – an inspection revealed a number of bent pushrods – and the transaxle failed on the second lap when the oil pump shaft sheared. With no spare transmission, the test was concluded. And Sebring's cyclone fence? Shelby's insurers paid out $91.95 for its replacement.

After the test, 1016 was sent to Charlotte where Holman & Moody's John Wanderer disassembled the car, re-engineered it to the team's own specification and prepared it for the Daytona 24 Hour Continental on 5/6 February, the first time that the race had been run twice-round-the-clock. The sister Holman & Moody Mk II, P/1031, for team leader Walt Hansgen and his young protégé Mark Donohue, arrived only a week before Daytona, so the crews were flat-out readying it.

John Holman

- Holman & Moody boss John Holman (left) oversaw Ford's successful NASCAR campaigns, and when Dearborn decided to win Le Mans at any cost, he was brought in to run three of the eight Mk IIs. He and Henry Ford II confer in the Le Mans paddock. *Mark Cole collection*

John Holman was the doyen of NASCAR stock car builders, a Nashville trucker-turned-engineer who had started in auto racing in the 1950s by crewing teams in Mexican road races. He set up his own race shop in Charlotte, North Carolina in 1956 to run Ford's NASCAR operation, but when Ford pulled out of racing for seven years under the Congress-enforced Detroit Resolution, he teamed up with former driver Ralph Moody to form Holman & Moody (or Holman-Moody, or Holman Moody, as the company sometimes termed itself).

When Ford returned to racing, Holman & Moody took them to 92 NASCAR race wins and two Grand National championships. During that time, Ford was also chasing the Le Mans 24 Hours title, and after two abortive attempts by FAV and Shelby to beat Ferrari, Holman & Moody and Alan Mann Racing were enlisted to join Shelby in a three-pronged assault at La Sarthe. John Holman was by now also preparing the Ford Falcons which contested European rallies.

Holman & Moody-built 427 NASCAR engines were used as the basis for the Ford GT40 Mk II, before Dearborn took over the build. Holman & Moody ran three cars in the 1966 Le Mans race, including 1016 which finished third behind the two Shelby Mk IIs.

At the start of 1967 the company was heavily involved in updating the Mk II to Mk IIB specification, using Holman's trademark roll-cages and fire systems, the bulk of the work carried out by Holman himself with team manager John Wanderer and chief engineer Wes Moss. 1016 was used to test the modifications, and run by Holman & Moody in the April Le Mans test with recording equipment to obtain engine and aero data.

In the 1967 Le Mans race, John Holman ran three of the new Mk IVs in tandem with three for Shelby; Shelby won with Dan Gurney/AJ Foyt, while Holman & Moody finished fourth with Bruce McLaren/Mark Donohue. With that, the company's involvement in Le Mans ended and it returned to building cars and engines for NASCAR until the early 1970s, when Ralph Moody left.

John Holman died of a heart attack in 1985 at the age of 57, but his son Lee took over, building engines for the legendary Wood Brothers, and remains in control of the company to this day, restoring GT40s, building continuation MK IIs, and providing parts and advice to today's owners.

Chapter 6
Daytona 24 Hours
5–6 February 1966

1966 saw the first Daytona 24 Hours – up until then, Daytona sports car races had been either 500km or 2,000km events – and no less than five Mk IIs were entered, three for Shelby and two for Holman & Moody.

The only similarity between Daytona and Le Mans was the race duration; one was a man-made high-speed oval with an infield section, the other a 13-km road course from which regular traffic was banished during race week. Daytona was run mid-winter, with almost 13 hours of cold night, while Le Mans was held close to mid-summer, with only five hours of real darkness.

In contrast to the flat airfield circuit at Sebring, Daytona was a banked oval with a road-racing infield. Aware of the challenge of Daytona's 31-degree banking, Holman & Moody fitted 1016 with its own Competition Proven adjustable stabiliser bars, together heavy-duty springs and shock-absorbers. 1016 had also been fitted with Ford's experimental T-43 hydraulic 'Power-shift' automatic transmission.

The drivers were Richie Ginther and Ronnie Bucknum. Californian Ginther, 35 and a family friend and Ferrari F1 teammate of Phil Hill, was a highly-rated development driver who had just come from a full Formula 1 season with Honda, winning the 1965 Mexican Grand Prix. Bucknum, 29 and a fellow Californian, had been the Japanese manufacturer's first driver in 1964, and Ginther's teammate throughout 1965.

Dan Gurney was making his Ford GT debut, driving Shelby's P/1012. The lanky Californian had won the GT class at Le Mans in 1964 in a Shelby Cobra. Because of his height, a bulge was put into the driver's door roof, and the 'Gurney Bubble' was born. This modification was quickly adopted by other tall drivers.

1016 ran with no.87 in the same white and black bodywork as at the Sebring tests, but with a Dayglo orange patch on the nose to tell it apart from the other Fords. It qualified sixth in the strong 60-car field which was headed by Ken Miles in no.98 Shelby Mk II and Jo Bonnier in the Chaparral 2D coupe. The Chaparral was powered by General Motors and also had an automatic transmission.

Despite the uprated suspension, 1016 wore through its front wheel arches on the banking during qualifying, and early in the race ran with a bubble patch on the right (the left was also to wear through and another patch was added). As a result, future front wheel arches would be more humped.

Ginther took the start, but was in the pits at the end of the first lap with brake failure; the master cylinder was quickly replaced, and he rejoined, rapidly clawing back positions. By 100 laps, the car was up to eighth, and at 120 laps it was running fifth. But at 4.20am, soon after the mid-race mark, the torque convertor failed on the automatic transmission, and 1016's race was finished.

Three of the five Mk IIs went on to make it an historic Ford 1-2-3, two Shelby cars (no.98 Ken Miles/Lloyd Ruby and no.97 Dan Gurney/Jerry Grant) from the Holman & Moody no.95 driven by Walt Hansgen and Mark Donohue, while the third Shelby no.96 Mk II of Bruce McLaren and Chris Amon car finished fifth.

The 1966 Daytona 24 Hours was first race for 1016 after its work as the Mk II development mule; this picture shows the Len Bailey slab nose, now used by all Ford GTs, and the wheel-arch bubble made after a tyre rubbed through on the banking.
LAT Images

Daytona 24 Hours

<u>TELETYPE REPORT ON THE DAYTONA 24-HOUR CONTINENTAL ROAD RACE
AT DAYTONA INTERNATIONAL SPEEDWAY, DAYTONA BEACH, FLA.</u>

Date: February 5-6, 1966

The 3 p.m. advisory from the weather bureau ....47 degrees...High 48....Low tonight (midnight) will be around 30-35 degrees. Wind North Northwest to Northeast at 15 to 16 miles per hour....occasional gusts up to 20 mph.

Here is a special bulletin from the race officials. The start of the race has been changed from the original plans. Cars will leave the grid and continue around the track once. On the second lap around entries will be given the green starting flag on the backstretch....cars will enter the infield road course on the first lap around. Reason for this change according to the steward of the meet was the safety factor involved.

<u>Starting Drivers in the Continental</u>

1	98	Miles	21	6	Guldstrand	41	54	Stoutenburg
2	65	Bonnier	22	20	Posey	42	19	Forlong
3	95	Hansgen	23	93	Keck	43	45	Byron
4	21	Rodriguez	24	16	Mitter	44	36	Ficket
5	25	Bianchi	25	89	Gerber	45	41	Kleinpeter
6	87	Ginther	26	17	Klass	46	7	Bolander
7	96	Amon	27	88	Wonder	47	55	Weaver
8	32	Follmer	28	14	Gregg	48	77	Bentley
9	28	Hulme	29	99	West	49	44	Croucher
10	91	Thompson	30	47	Lane	50	43	Kelder
11	97	Gurney	31	12	Hull	51	73	McKemie
12	27	Piper	32	23	Konig	52	42	Hughes
13	31	Fulp	33	30	Perkins	53	5	May
14	22	Rindt	34	90	Kearney	54	56	Maxwell
15	92	Revson	35	94	Noseda	55	84	Scott
16	24	Ireland	36	79	Richards	56	40	Waltman
17	29	Hawkins	37	75	Reiley	57	80	Mims
18	15	Herrmann	38	67	Cornelius	58	78	Smith
19	86	Sutcliffe	39	18	Ryan	59	74	L. Hess
20	26	Denier	40	59	Yenko	60	85	Clark

Chapparal led first lap. Ford Mk II took lead on second lap with Miles driving.
No. 87 out on first lap....master cylinder
No. 47 in pits....overheating
Ferrari GTC No. 47 came in to check plugs
Chapparal in pits on lap 7 running second at time. Chapparal back in race on lap 11. Reason for stop...fan belt loose and hitting back of seat.
No.87 Repaired brake cylinder and is back in race.

- Official race reports show that No 87 – 1016 – was the first car to pit, when the brake master cylinder failed on the first lap. It climbed back to fifth before the torque converter failed on the auto-box at 4.20 am Sunday. Its sister cars went on to an historic 1-2-3.

TELETYPE REPORT (CONTINENTAL) Page 2

No. 59 out for 16 laps - radiator trouble
No. 12 fuel - Hull driving
No. 45 fuel - Byrne driving
5 P.M. RUNDOWN.....2 HOURS....SPEED 109.21 MPH
98 95 21 97 25 91 96 27 22 31
All protos except No. 91 (sports)
No. 9 Driver change - Reina - fuel
No. 88 Driver change-Wentanson - fuel
No. 27 fuel, oil
No. 18 Driver change - Coleman - fuel
No. 47 Overheating
No. 43 driver change - Dube - fuel
No. 19 Driver change - Dieas -
No. 14 driver change - Drolsom
No. 89 driver change - Lerch
No. 77 engine missing on turns
No. 75 driver change - MacGrotty
Chapparal back in race on lap 63
Bonnier driving cgapparal
No. 21 driver change - Andretti
No. 30 driver change - Slottag
No. 26 driver change - Dernier - fuel
No. 27 Electrical system trouble
No. 98 The leader in pits on lap no. 76 -out after fuel only in same lap
No. 26 Driver change - Icks (that is the correct spelling)
6 P.M. RUNDOWN......THREE HOURS 98 95 97 25 31
No. 74 Fuel and a tire
No. 77 Driver change - Bentley
No. 32 driver change - Wester
No. 28 Out of race - transmission and axel
No. 96 the 3th place car pitted for fuel and tires
No. 42 Driver change - Salo
No. 36 Driver change-Bean
No. 95 driver change - Hansgen - fuel
RUNDOWN AT END OF 100 LAPS SPEED 109.12 MPH
98 95 97 31 25 21 91 87 22 96 27
Interesting Note: Chapparal is back out and turning laps in excess of 114 MPH
Grant now driving No. 97
Allison driving No. 5
No. 24 out of race with transmission trouble
No. 91 Driver change - Thompson
No. 99 driver change - West
No. 89 Driver change - Johnson
No. 23 driver change - Clark
No. 21 driver change - Rodriguez
No. 21 change of tires
No. 90 driver change - Kearney
No. 31 in pits because driver said that it didn't sound right. Is now back on the course.
Top three in each class
GRAND TOURING 86 6 99
PROTOTYPE 98 97 95
SPORTS 91 92 16
RUNDOWN AT 120 laps ... SPEED 108.32 MPH
98 97 95 25 87 96 22 21 31 91
No. 31 Ferrari has a broken wheel bearing
No. 98 leader Miles stopped at 7:20 for gas and tires
No. 20 Ferrari is out of the race with transmission problems at 7:18 p.m.
Car No. 80 is now being driven by Guthrie
RUNDOWN AT 133 LAPS....SPEED 109.28 MPH
95 98 97 25 96 21 22 87 91
No. 25 Ferrari-change tires
Report on the Chapparal.....Last stop was for gas and oil also replaced exhaust pipe. Had a hole in it and they were afraid of fire.
Car No. 95, the leader stooped for gas oil and tires at 8:15 p.m. New leader is Car no. 98 Miles and Ruby.
Car No. 95 stopped on lap 118 for a scheduled stop for gas, etc. Donohue is now driving

Running in the black and white livery used for the Sebring tests, 1016 now had an orange dayglow nose patch for night identification. The Bailey nose transformed the front-aerodynamics, and the MK II was now a well-balanced race car.
The Henry Ford/Dave Friedman

Pit stop for 1012 in the midnight chill; the Holman & Moody crew refuel and change the Goodyear tyres; by now a crossover refuelling system, enabling them to fill both pontoon tanks from one side, was installed, but it still took 68 seconds.
LAT Images

Daytona 24 Hours

Richie Ginther in 1016 leads the No. 92 Essex Wire GT40 of fellow Americans Peter Revson, Masten Gregory and Ed Lowther off the North Banking. Unlike Ginther and Bucknum, they would finish, but in a delayed 17th place.
LAT Images

Ronnie Bucknum passes the Ecurie Francorchamps Ferrari 365 P2 of Lucien Bianchi, Jean Blaton and Gerard Langlois von Ophem on the high side. Ecurie Francorchamps, the team of Belgian Ferrari dealer Jacques Swaters, was a leading Maranello privateer.
LAT Images

1966 Daytona 24 Hours (USA) 5-6 February
Round 1 International Manufacturers' Championship

1 Ken Miles (GB)/Lloyd Ruby (USA) Ford Mk II (1015) 678 laps	
2 Dan Gurney (USA)/Jerry Grant (USA) Ford Mk II (1012) 670 laps	
3 Walt Hansgen (USA)/Mark Donohue (USA) Ford Mk II (1031) 669 laps	
4 Pedro Rodriguez (MEX)/Mario Andretti (USA) Ferrari 365P2/3 664 laps	
5 Chris Amon (NZ)/Bruce McLaren (NZ) Ford Mk II (1011) 651 laps	
6 Hans Herrmann (D)/Herbert Linge (D) Porsche 906 623 laps	
7 Gerhard Mitter (D)/Joe Buzzetta (USA) Porsche 904GTS 612 laps	
8 Guenther Klass (D)/Udo Schütz (D) Porsche 904GTS 610 laps	
9 Jochen Rindt (A)/Bob Bondurant (USA) Ferrari 250LM 591 laps	
10 Peter Gregg (USA)/George Drolsom (USA) Porsche 904GTS 589 laps	

DNF Richie Ginther (USA)/Ronnie Bucknum (USA) Ford Mk II (1016) 329 laps transmission

Richie Ginther

- Californian Ginther was a talented engineer as well as a grand prix-winning driver. He grew up with Phil Hill and worked on the future world champion's cars before starting to race himself.
  The Revs Institute for Automotive Research/Max Le Grand

- It was Ginther's development work on the 1.5-litre 156 shark-nose that gave Ferrari a world-beating Formula 1 car; it took seven grand prix victories and the 1961 world title for Phil Hill, while Ginther scored three podium places.
  The Revs Institute for Automotive Research/George Phillips

Coast Ferrari importer Luigi Chinetti, who in 1957 entered him for both Sebring and Le Mans.

Between then and 1960, he was regularly winning US races for Ferrari, and when the call came from Maranello, the American signed for the factory's Formula 1 team in 1960, alongside Hill and Wolfgang von Trips. He finished sixth at Monaco and Zandvoort, and ended the year second in the Italian GP, behind Hill. In 1961 he was second at Monaco, and twice third, at Spa and Silverstone, in the beautiful shark-nosed 156, which he had largely developed. But Ferrari, he later told *Motor Sport,* 'was a joke, they gave me $400 a month, and when I left for BRM, *Il Commendatore* wouldn't even let me say goodbye to my mechanics.'

At BRM, he partnered another Hill, Graham, not only in Formula 1 but also at the 1964 Le Mans 24 Hours in the innovative Rover-BRM gas turbine car; 00 finished the race eighth overall, although not officially classified as it was the only car in its category. As a proven development driver, able to give accurate feedback to the team, in 1963 he scored five F1 podium finishes (two of them second places, at Monza and Watkins Glen) to finish the season third in the world

Richie Ginther's moment in history was when he won the 1965 Mexican Grand Prix, giving Honda – and Japan – a first Formula 1 victory, the precursor of many to follow. His older brother was a friend of Phil Hill, who was raised in the same town of Granada Hills, California and it was Hill who gave him his first taste of racing when he helped the future world champion prepare and race his own cars.

Leaving school in 1948, he had gone to work for Douglas Aircraft where he learned his mechanical skills, until he was drafted for national service in Korea. On returning, still with his trademark crew-cut, he joined Hill as co-driver in two editions of the Carrera Panamericana across Mexico; they crashed in the 1953 race, but finished second to Ferrari works driver Umberto Maglioli in 1954. Ginther started racing himself, in Austin-Healeys, and then for a West Coast Ferrari dealer; the latter caught the attention of East

Ginther in the bulky 1966 3-litre Honda R273 on his way to fourth place in the Mexican GP; a year earlier in Mexico he had taken the R272 to the Japanese manufacturer's first win, in the last race of the 1.5-litre Formula 1 era.
The Revs Institute for Automotive Research/Max Le Grand

championship, behind team leader Hill.

After finishing fourth in the standings for BRM in 1964, he was head-hunted by Honda, and signed for 1965 alongside Ronnie Bucknum, who had helped develop the first Honda F1 car during 1964. The RS272 was as fragile as its predecessor, but by the end of the season Ginther had improved it enough to give it a first win in Mexico City, the last race of the 1.5-litre Formula 1 era.

Honda took a six-month sabbatical while it readied its 3-litre car, the RA273, so Bucknum suggested to Ford that Ginther join him for the 1966 Daytona 24 Hours, where they shared Holman & Moody's 1016. Like Jim Hall's Chaparral 2D, 1016 had an automatic transmission mated to the 7-litre V8, which at first delivered the goods, but after qualifying sixth and running fifth in the race, the torque converter failed.

Ginther was not to race sports cars again, but returned to Honda for the second half of 1966, after driving a Cooper-Maserati in the early F1 season. He broke his collarbone when he crashed the Honda at Monza whilst leading, but recovered enough to finish fourth in the Mexico season finale.

A move to Dan Gurney's Anglo American Eagle team followed, but having qualified 16th for the Monaco GP behind Gurney, he was controversially bumped off the 16-car grid by the Formula 2 Matra of Johnny Servoz-Gavin, which had been weighted up to F1 specification to give a French interest in the race. Disillusioned, Ginther quit Formula 1 there and then.

He died of a heart attack whilst on holiday with his family in Bordeaux in 1989, aged 59. Phil Hill's tribute at his funeral said everything about his skills: 'We were on the Ferrari team at the same time, and Richie did a tremendous job of helping to develop the new Formula One cars.'

Ronnie Bucknum

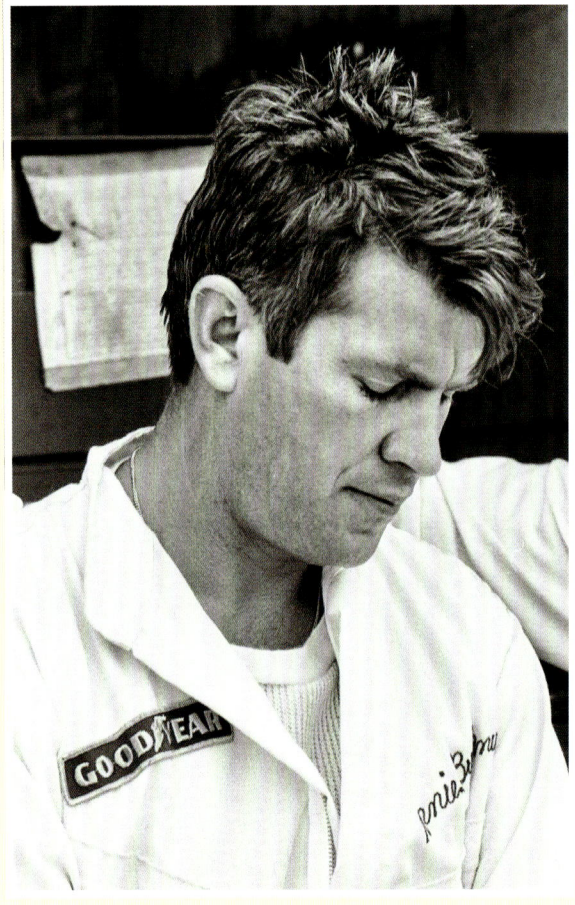

Ronnie Bucknum, like Ginther, had been a successful sports car racer, headhunted by Honda for its fledgling F1 programme. Holman & Moody later spotted his talent for their Le Mans squad.
Claude Nahum collection/ Gerard Crombac

Californian Ronnie Bucknum came to fame as a West Coast Porsche champion, the trainee surveyor winning 52 of his 56 races during a four year sweep of SCCA titles between 1959 and 1964. Honda was planning on going Formula 1 racing when its engineers spotted him in action in a Porsche 904 at Sebring, and chose him to head their fledgling Grand Prix programme, even though he had never so much as sat in a single-seater.

Bucknum and Honda learned F1 together, and he was to make 11 starts in the 1.5-litre V12 RA271, debuting at the Nürburgring in 1964, where he qualified last and then spun out of the race. Retirements followed in its only other two races, the Italian and United States GPs.

Despite breaking a leg in a testing crash at Suzuka prior to the 1965 season, for which he was to be joined by fellow Californian Richie Ginther, he took the RA272 to 13th in the 1965 German GP, and then to 5th in Mexico. This was the last race of the 1.5-litre formula, at which Ginther claimed Honda and Goodyear's first F1 win.

Honda's 3-litre RA273 would not be ready for the start of the 1966 season, so Ford was able to call on him and Ginther for its third attempt to win Le Mans; both tested the Holman Moody Mk II 1016 at Sebring prior to the Daytona 24 Hours, collecting valuable data. At Daytona, the automatic transmission uniquely fitted to their car failed after 12 hours.

But Ginther was then called to the Cooper F1 team, so for the Sebring 12 Hours, fellow American and two-times Indy 500 winner AJ Foyt was paired with Bucknum. This time the auto-box held together but, after several brake pad changes, they were classified only 12th.

Bucknum, now 29, was originally scheduled to be partnered by Foyt for the Le Mans 24 Hours in June, but AJ had suffered burns in an Indycar crash, so he was joined by Holman & Moody-contracted NASCAR racer Dick Hutcherson, who was currently without a drive whilst Ford was taking a sabbatical from NASCAR. Together they helped the Blue Oval to sweep the board in France with third place in 1016, ending Ferrari's six-year winning streak.

At this point, Honda's second RA273 was ready for what was left of the 1966 Formula 1 season, and while Bucknum posted a retirement in the US Grand Prix, he finished eighth in Mexico. For 1967, Honda dropped both him and Ginther in favour of its former motorcycle world champion John Surtees.

Bucknum then looked to Indycar racing, but was to return to Le Mans for a second time with Ford in 1967, this time in a Shelby Mk IIB with Paul Hawkins. They led the first hour from Ford's winning Mk IV, before a cracked water pipe cost them two hours in the pits, then a dropped valve ended their race after 18 hours.

He had his one and only Indycar win at Michigan in 1968, and then concentrated on TransAm with Roger Penske's team. He was to race for a third time at Le Mans in 1970, when he and Sam Posey took Luigi Chinetti's Ferrari 512S to fourth place overall. His biggest sports car success, however, was yet to come: second place in the 1971 Daytona 24 Hours, in that same Ferrari with Tony Adamowicz, beaten only by the Gulf Porsche 917 of Pedro Rodriguez/Jackie Oliver.

He died in 1992, aged 56, from diabetes, but his son Jeff carried on the family tradition, racing at Le Mans in 2003, and in 2005 driving for Foyt's Indycar team.

Bucknum's place in history was assured when he debuted Honda's first Formula 1 entry, the RA271, in the 1964 German GP at the Nürburgring. Neither Ronnie nor Honda had any previous F1 experience; he spun out of the race.
The Revs Institute for Automotive Research/Eric della Faille

Daytona 24 Hours

Ford GT40 MkII 1016

Chapter 7
Sebring 12 Hours
26 March 1966

The Sebring 12 Hours was a Saturday race run on 26 March, the start of the college Spring Break, which always attracted big crowds to the central Florida track. 1016 was entered for Bucknum and two-times Indy 500 winner AJ Foyt, replacing Ginther who was now driving for Cooper in Formula 1. The car had by now received its own bodywork, gold with a matt-black anti-glare hood, sporting no.4.

Following a further power hike after Daytona (to 471bhp at 6,400rpm), brakes continued to be an issue, so for Sebring, brake-cooling snorkels were fitted to the rear decks of all the Mark IIs. For this race, Shelby entered Daytona winners Ken Miles and Lloyd Ruby in the X-1, an aluminium-chassis open-top Ford GT Roadster, prepared for Can-Am by McLaren Racing in England with a 427 engine.

Tech inspection was in Sebring town centre, with the cars driven the three miles from the track to give the local population and racegoers a close look at the entry. 1016 was again fitted with the automatic gearbox which had let it down at Daytona. The X-1 also started race week with an auto-box but after two breakages in practice, Miles had the T-44 transaxle retro-fitted.

The two-speed auto, while saving on constant manual shifts, lacked acceleration, and in qualifying Bucknum, paid the price: he was 10th on the grid. The Chaparrals were similarly disadvantaged, in sixth and eighth places. In the race, neither Chaparral made it past the two-hour mark with oil issues, while both Holman & Moody cars were struggling with brake problems, calling for frequent pit-stops. John Wanderer mused, 'by the end of the race none of us could recall how many sets of pads we'd changed'.

Miles and Ruby in the X-1 headed a Ford 1-2-3 from the Hansgen/Donohue Holman & Moody Mk II (P/1031) and the Peter Revson/Skip Scott Essex Wire GT40. Leader Dan Gurney's engine blew on the final lap, and he was disqualified for pushing his Shelby car over the finish line.

Despite their problems, both Holman & Moody cars finished. Bucknum and Foyt were 12th with 1016, proving that the automatic transmission could survive a rough-and-tumble 12 hour race on a circuit which, even today, drivers say is harder than 24 hours at Le Mans.

The post-race inquest pointed to braking issues for the Holman & Moody cars: boiling brake fluid in the no.3 car and a jammed brake balance bar on no. 4. In addition, 1016 had clogged filters in the Stewart Warner fuel pumps which dropped the pressure, and twice lost rear wheel balance weights due to interference with the brake-cooling ducts.

The two American races were a part of the Triple Crown shared with the Le Mans 24 Hours – Ford had won both, and both with Shelby winning and Holman & Moody in second and third places. Could they do the same again in France?

As one journal wrote, 'For Ford, the balance of the two American endurance races was extremely positive, it was now fully-proven that new Mk IIA prototypes and the spyder GT-XI were absolutely reliable. The test with the automatic gearbox on the no.4 Ford Mk IIA let see that the approach was too experimental to try such an adventure at Le Mans.'

A livery change for 1016 at the 1966 Sebring 12 Hours, where it again ran with the Ford T-43 two-speed auto box, with a power increase to 471bhp; Lloyd Ruby's laid-back driving style is evident as he negotiates the Hairpin.
LAT Images

Sebring 12 Hours

● Now gold, although with a non-reflective matt black front, 1016 going through scrutineering in the centre of Sebring, where everyone had the chance to see cars and drivers up close.
Claude Nahum collection/ Rich Leuchner

● Sebring attests its airfield origins as 1016 races past parked aircraft in the 1966 12 Hours; as Hendricks Army Airfield it was a B17 bomber training base from 1941.
Claude Nahum collection/ Gerard Crombac

● Despite numerous stops for brake pad and disc changes, 1016 finished its second race in 12th place on a bumpy track which is harder on cars than Le Mans. H&M crew chief John Wanderer lost count of how many sets they got through.
Claude Nahum collection

Sebring 12 Hours

- Night-time pit stop for 1016 as Ronnie Bucknum gets instructions; this time the auto transmission held out, although a catalogue of other problems kept the car out of the top 10. Its sister H&M manual gearbox car finished third.
Claude Nahum collection

- Spectator safety was an issue at the 1966 race; four in a restricted area were killed when Mario Andretti's Ferrari and a Porsche 906 collided. In a separate crash, Canadian Bob McLean also died when his privateer GT40 hit a pole and caught fire.
Claude Nahum collection/ Gerard Crombac

1966 Sebring 12 Hours (USA) 26 March
Round 2 International Manufacturers' Championship

1	Ken Miles (GB)/Lloyd Ruby (USA)	Ford X-1 Roadster (110)	228 laps
2	Walt Hansgen (USA)/Mark Donohue (USA)	Ford Mk II (1032)	216 laps
3	Skip Scott (USA) /Peter Revson (USA)	Ford GT40 (1026)	213 laps
4	Hans Herrmann (D)/Joe Buzzetta (USA)	Porsche 906	209 laps
5	Ludovico Scarfiotti (I)/Lorenzo Bandini (I)	Ferrari Dino 206P	206 laps
6	Jo Siffert (CH)/Charles Voegele (CH)	Porsche 906	206 laps
7	George Follmer (USA)/Peter Gregg (USA)	Porsche 904GTS	205 laps
8	Lake Underwood (USA)/Ed Hugus (USA)	Porsche 906	204 laps
9	George Wintersteen (USA)/Ben Moore (USA)	Chevrolet Corvette	201 laps
10	Bob Grossman (USA)/Ed Lowther (USA)	Shelby Cobra	197 laps
12	**Ronnie Bucknum (USA) /AJ Foyt (USA)**	**Ford Mk II (1016)**	**192 laps**

Sebring 12 Hours

● The GT40-based X-1 Roadster was built by McLaren for Can-Am, but won at Sebring when the Chaparrals went out with oil leaks, giving Ken Miles and Lloyd Ruby their second successive win for the Blue Oval.
The Revs Institute for Automotive Research/Albert Bochroch

AJ Foyt

- AJ Foyt remains America's greatest driver, winning in every discipline in which he raced. Le Mans and Daytona 24 Hours, Sebring 12 Hours, Indy and Daytona 500s all figure on his winning CV. But he was to miss Le Mans 1966 after an Indycar crash.
Claude Nahum collection/Gerard Crombac

Known to all as 'AJ', Anthony Joseph Foyt is America's most successful racing driver. To this day, he is the only driver to have claimed the triple crown of the Le Mans 24 Hours, the Daytona 24 Hours and the Sebring 12 Hours, and to win both the Indianapolis 500 and Daytona 500, a multi-disciplined achievement no-one is likely to ever match.

Born in Houston, Texas in 1935, he started racing in midgets at the age of 18, before graduating to sprint cars – taking the 1960 USAC championship with 28 wins - then Champ Cars. He won both the 1960 and 1961 Champ Car titles; one of his eight wins was the 1961 Indianapolis 500. He repeated the title double in 1963 and 1964 with 16 wins, taking his second Indy 500 in 1964. A fifth Champ Car title followed in 1967 along with his third Indy 500 victory, and he added his sixth and seventh championships in 1975 and 1979. His fourth and final Indy 500 win was in 1977.

He also enjoyed a 33-year NASCAR career, both as driver and entrant, although his five wins all came early, between 1970 and 1972 with Mercury and the fabled Wood Brothers, one of them the 1972 Daytona 500.

Sports car racing came almost as an afterthought, although Ford was keen to have him on board from 1966, when he was rostered to share 1016 at Sebring with Ronnie Bucknum. This was the only Mk II to have the two-speed auto-box, which had failed at Daytona seven weeks previously, and although it continued to give problems, they did at least finish 12th.

Prior to Le Mans, AJ had crashed in an Indycar race at the Milwaukee Mile, suffering burns, so had to miss the French race, in which Ford finished 1-2-3. But Ford had not given up on him, and he was retained for their 1967 sports car programme. Pole position at the Daytona 24 Hours, sharing with Dan Gurney, ended with engine failure after a mid-race gearbox change.

At Sebring, he and Lloyd Ruby lost the chance of victory when a broken camshaft left them sitting in the pits for the final 30 minutes, although their Mk IIB was still classified second behind Bruce McLaren and Mario Andretti in the new Mk IV.

In June, Foyt was paired with Gurney for Le Mans, and the two Americans took their red Mk IV to Ford's second successive win in the French classic, beating the sole surviving factory Ferrari by four laps after a trouble-free run. Well, it was almost trouble-free; Gurney reputedly overslept during the night, and AJ had to double-stint, without losing the lead. He ended up driving almost 16 of the 24 hours: 'It wasn't so hard', he said, 'Indy is harder.'

Asked about their winning drive, AJ said, 'I think Dan and I had the same idea, we knew we couldn't tear the car all to pieces. We knew we had to take care of it. We had to nurse it, then when we had to run hard, we could run hard. I think that's how we won the race.'

Foyt had not endeared himself to the French before the race by referring to the La Sarthe circuit as 'nothin' but a little old country road', and then on the podium asked officials if he was due the 'Rookie of the Year award' for having won Le Mans on his debut. It was also the first and, to date, the only all-American victory in the race: entrant, car and drivers.

He went on to race sports cars again, winning the Daytona 24 Hours with Bob Wollek for Preston Henn Porsche in 1983 and 1985, and the Sebring 12 Hours, again with Wollek, in 1985. AJ retired from driving in the mid-1990s, but continues as an Indycar team owner to this day.

- AJ takes his Offenhauser-powered Indy roadster to victory in the 1964 Indy 500, the last time a front-engined car would win. The writing had been on the Brickyard wall since 1963, when Jim Clark drove a mid-engined Lotus-Ford to second place.
Getty Images

Sebring 12 Hours

Chapter 8
Le Mans 24 Hours
18-19 June 1966

The European season started in April in the worst of circumstances for the Ford factory team. Walt Hansgen, the runner-up at Sebring, was killed at the Le Mans Test Weekend when his Holman & Moody Mk II aquaplaned up the escape road at the end of the pits straight and hit a pile of construction sand which should never have been there; terribly injured, he died five days later. In the aftermath, the factory withdrew from the Monza 1,000Km which was won by the Ferrari 330P3 of John Surtees and Mike Parkes.

As it had never intended to go to the Nürburgring 1,000Km, Ford's final chance to prepare under race conditions for Le Mans was at the Spa 1,000Km on 22 May. One 7-litre Mk II, delivered to Alan Mann Racing, was entered along with six GT40s. Driven by Sir John Whitmore and Frank Gardner, the Mk II finished second to Ferrari. Strong winds affected the Ford more than the Ferrari but the five-hour race did show that the Mk II was now reasonably reliable.

1016, with the Sebring test and two races under its belt, went back to Charlotte to be readied for Le Mans. A complete rebuild in early April included a change to a T-44 manual gearbox (KKL-123), and a new engine (AX316-1-143); the 427s, with further refinements during hours of dyno testing, were now showing up to 500bhp at 6,800rpm, although there was a 36hp disparity between the best and the worst. Whilst still gold (the black nose had gone), the car now had white Ford door stripes, and the headlight surrounds were white under the Plexiglass covers.

A test at Riverside was pencilled for 17 May, just a month before Le Mans, but that was changed to 30 May at Virginia International Raceway, where both Holman & Moody entries ran. NASCAR driver Dick Hutcherson drove 1016 over 67 laps, learning the car. Donohue ran P/1032 over 72 laps, and both bedded-in multiple sets of quick-change brake pads and discs. Apart from an oil gasket leak on 1016, there were no further problems, and both cars were loaded for shipment to New York, to join the third Holman & Moody entry, P/1031. Then it was on to Paris, together with a 40-foot trailer kitted out as a mobile race shop.

Hutcherson, 34, from Iowa, was one of Ford's NASCAR stars, having finished runner-up for Holman & Moody in the 1965 Grand National championship. But Ford briefly withdrew from NASCAR in 1966, so as a Ford-contracted driver he was seconded to the Le Mans programme, although was missing off the ACO driver roster – AJ Foyt had been listed to share with Bucknum.

Hutch's chance came when Foyt was burned in a crash at the Milwaukee Mile Indycar race. Lloyd Ruby was in hospital after an accident in a light aircraft, so there were changes at both the Shelby and Holman & Moody teams. Alan Mann was a driver short too, after Jackie Stewart, who had driven a Mann GT40 at Sebring, was injured at the Belgian Grand Prix.

Ford was determined to beat Ferrari after two failures and had asked John Wyer to use his ACO connections to try to obtain 15 entries for Le Mans. After some French horse-trading, he was able to secure 13 for Ford – eight factory Mk IIs, and five privateer GT40 Mk Is, plus one reserve.

The Mk IIs were spread among Shelby American (three), Holman & Moody (three) and Alan Mann (two),

Days of glory: 1016 in a rare moment of sunshine during the 1966 Le Mans 24 Hours, Ronnie Bucknum is at the wheel. The car now had the same Ford T-44 manual gearbox as the rest of the Mk IIs, but its pink dayglo patches picked it out from the rest.
The Henry Ford/Dave Friedman

Le Mans 24 Hours

Le Mans 24 Hours

● Ford took over half of a Le Mans Peugeot dealer's workshops to prepare the eight factory cars among 27 tons of spares and even Transit vans. 1016 is between Nos. 4 and 6. Note, in background, Peugeot 404 road cars being serviced. *Ford*

neatly numbered 1 to 8, They were up against seven factory Ferraris.

Ford had bought 27 tons of freight to support its eight-car attack, including elaborate work-benches, machine tools, and even coffee and Coca-Cola machines. It had rented half of the workshop space at a Le Mans Peugeot dealership for its three factory teams; the Mk IIs were prepared alongside customer Peugeot 404s in for service.

John Holman had brought in the legendary Wood Brothers NASCAR crew to help his team. 1016's final

After a leak in qualifying for ● 1031, all three Holman & Moody cars had the fuel bag-tanks changed for Firestone cells; those for 1016 await insertion into the under-door pontoons, a difficult job at the best of times. *Claude Nahum collection*

Le Mans 24 Hours

LETTER NO. 34337 From L'Automobile-Club de L'Ouest
Dated June 1, 1966

"With reference to your entry in the 34th 24-hour Grand Prix of Endurance & Performance, taking place on June 18 & 19, may we inform you:

1. That your entry, Ford, 427 CID, which will be driven by **Ronnie Bucknum** and **A. J. Foyt** has been assigned the Car Number **# 5**. (Car Serial # **1016**, Crew Chief, **Bobby Auman**.

2. That the drivers must be with their car

2. That, according to Article 43 of the general rules, you are requested to have your car, with the drivers and mechanics, for scrutineering and weighing: Date: Tues. June 14 Time: 1500 (3:00 PM)

3. That the drivers must be with the car.

4. That the deadline for inspection is Wednesday, June 15th, at 1600 (4:00 PM) and that any car not inspected by that time, may not be admitted to the race.

May we remind you that customs declaration documents must accompany the car of foreign entry.

ATTENTION: Inspection will take place at the race course, in the enclosed park located across from the Time Keepers Stand. (Use entrance on Boulevard des Italiens, adjacent to the air field.)

May we remind you that because of the complexity of inspection, a car presented late will have to remain at the disposition of the inspectors as long as necessary, so that it can be inspected, if possible, at a time other than previously assigned for the different operation consequently. There will be a penalty of 100 Francs.

Your cooperation in this matter will help inspection and eliminate the possibility of penalties.

Thank you.

R. A'cat
Le Secrétaire Général de l'A.C.O.

COMPETITION & DEVELOPMENT DIVISION --- MOVEMENT SCHEDULE
The 34th Grand Prix of Endurance -- 24 Hours of Le Mans, June 18 and 19, 1966

CARS & DRIVERS

Car & Chassis No.	Engine No.	Drivers	Company Responsible
GT40P-1015	AX-316-1-148	Ken Miles / Lloyd Ruby	S. A. I.
GT40P-1046	AX-316-1-141	Chris Amon / Bruce McLaren	S. A. I.
GT40P-1047	AX-316-1-142	Dan Gurney / Jerry Grant	S. A. I.
GT40P-1016	AX-316-1-143	Mark Donohue / Paul Hawkins	H. & M.
GT40P-1031	AX-316-1-144	Lucien Bianchi / Mario Andretti	H. & M.
GT40P-1032	AX-316-1-149	A. J. Foyt / Ronnie Bucknum	H. & M.
XGT-1	AX-316-1-145	John Whitmore / Frank Gardner	Alan Mann
XGT-2	AX-316-1-147	Jackie Stewart / Graham Hill	Alan Mann

EXTRA DRIVERS:
Shelby American -- Dick Thompson
Holman & Moody -- Bob Grossman
Alan Mann -- Denny Hulme

EXTRA CARS:
GT40P-1012   AX-316-1-150
XGT-3

TRANSPORTATION:

Chassis: 1015) 1046) 1047) - Scheduled to depart Los Angeles via TWA on June 1st for Paris.

X-1) X-2) - Scheduled to depart Los Angeles via TWA on June 2nd for London.

1031 - Scheduled to depart Los Angeles via TWA on June 5th for Paris.

1032) 1013) - Scheduled to meet #1031 in New York June 6th and all three will then proceed to Paris.

● The Automobile Club de l'Ouest confirmation of 1016's entry, given No 5; but after AJ Foyt was burned at Milwaukee, reserve driver Dick Hutcherson was drafted in. Ford's movement memo originally assigned 1016 to Donohue and Hawkins.

● Late afternoon in the pits for a photo-shoot sees the six Shelby and Holman & Moody cars before they had their colour patches added to ease identification. The Mk IIs were painted in Ford range colours at the behest of the marketing department. *Claude Nahum collection*

Le Mans 24 Hours

Le Mans 24 Hours

● 4pm Saturday, and Henry Ford II has flagged the 34th Grand Prix d'Endurance away, drivers having sprinted to their cars and fired up, many starting with belts unfastened. The iconic chevron start would be discontinued in 1970 on safety grounds.
Claude Nahum collection

driver line-up was settled as Bucknum/Hutcherson, with Bobby Auman as crew chief. Bob Grossman was listed as the reserve driver for the three Holman & Moody entries but was not required.

During the two days of practice and qualifying, 1016 underwent a number of detail changes; the white headlight backgrounds were replaced by black, pink dayglo identification patches were applied across the nose and on the pit-facing rear door pillar, and the brake cooling snorkels used at Sebring were re-installed. It was also given a driver's door 'Gurney Bubble' to accommodate the tall Hutcherson.

An in-house Holman & Moody memo reveals that all three cars had a 2.70-1 final drive to better suit the long, fast La Sarthe circuit, and that 1016 had suspension adjustments made to improve handling characteristics. Further sets of brake discs were run-in, and a cooling duct added to blow air on to the drivers' feet. There was

Le Mans 24 Hours

Moments later, Graham Hill has put his XGT-2 – the Alan Mann-built Mk II - into the lead from Ronnie Bucknum in 1016, with pole-man Dan Gurney immediately behind.
The Klemantaski Collection/ Nigel Snowdon

a fuel cell leak in P/1031, so the cells on all three cars were replaced with Firestone units.

In practice, Dick Thompson driving an Alan Mann Mk II collided with Richard Holqvist's dawdling privateer GT40, which was destroyed. The ACO ruled that as he had not officially reported the accident, it disqualified the car he was sharing with Graham Hill. Outraged, Ford, supported by Porsche, threatened to withdrew their entries, forcing a *volte face* by the organisers;

Thompson was excluded, but the car could race, with Australian Brian Muir brought in to partner Hill. Muir had some experience of the 427, having driven the Willment Galaxie in British touring car races.

After the two days and nights of qualifying, Ford had swept the board with a 1-2-3-4 for the Shelby cars of Gurney and Miles, Frank Gardner third for Alan Mann Racing, and McLaren fourth for Shelby, ahead of the best Ferrari, the 330 P2/3 of Pedro Rodriguez. The

Le Mans 24 Hours

- Early evening, and NASCAR star Dick Hutcherson powers 1016 through The Esses; note the 'Gurney bulge' in the door to accommodate his 6ft 4in height, and the pair of rear-deck snorkels to aid much-needed rear brake cooling.
Claude Nahum collection

- Hutcherson laps the Panhard CD Peugeot of Claude Laurent, one of many French aerodynamic specials built for Le Mans, which could reach 250km/h with just 108bhp! Further back, a gaggle of cars exits White House.
Claude Nahum collection

three Holman & Moody cars lined up ninth (Bucknum and Hutcherson in 1016, no.5), 11th (no.4 Donohue/Hawkins), and 12th (no.6 Bianchi/Andretti). 1016 was on Goodyear tyres, the other two on Firestones.

Gurney's pole time on 3min 30.6sec was a new record, 1.1 seconds quicker than team-mate Miles, and 2.4 sec better than the Ferrari. Shelby had also split its cars between Goodyear and Firestone. This was to have dramatic consequences as Firestone could offer only dry or full-wet tyres and a track that was to be damp for much of the race called for intermediates. With the Mk IIs hitting 220mph on the Mulsanne straight, the Firestone 'wets' were chunking, a problem the Goodyear runners did not have with their 'inters'.

There was a rain shower 20 minutes before the start-time, giving the teams a tyre dilemma. By 4pm when the French national flag was dropped by Henry Ford II, who had been named Honorary Starter, the sun was out and the track almost dry. Alan Mann's Ford Mark IIs were first away from the traditional Le Mans 'run and jump' start: Sir John Whitmore was the first to move but his engine stalled and it was Graham Hill who led on the track.

By the end of the first lap, Graham Hill led from Gurney and Bucknum, with Parkes fourth for Ferrari. Miles had to pit to have his driver door refitted after dislodging it when he slammed it on to his helmet.

After 80 minutes the sunshine turned to heavy rain, which brought cars into the pits for wet-weather tyres at the precise moment that others (Bucknum in 1016 among them) were refuelling. Bianchi, Hawkins and Hill were all sent off for another lap until there was space to service them.

Early Sunday morning: 1016 in the pits as the Holman & Moody crew check tyres and brakes. Bucknum ran 191 laps during the race to Hutcherson's 157, 1016 making a total of 16 pits stops with 10 driver changes. *Claude Nahum collection*

Le Mans 24 Hours

● Chased by the Pedro Rodriguez Ferrari P2/3, Dick Hutcherson prepares to pass the much-modified Austin-Healey Sprite of Andrew Hedges. The little British car outlasted the Ferraris 'which we ran into the ground', said Hutch.
Claude Nahum collection

● Fuel goes into 1016 as a rear Goodyear is changed, while Bucknum briefs his tall co-driver Hutcherson on track conditions. Shirt-sleeved John Holman sits on the pit counter, stopwatch in hand, feeling increasingly confident about Ford's chances.
Claude Nahum collection

Last of the Fords to pit was Bruce McLaren, who had started on Firestone tyres to honour his personal contract, but he was calling for Goodyears as the Firestones were breaking up. During the chaos, Ferrari had edged into the lead, but Gurney and Bucknum quickly regained the head of the field, no.5 (1016) running strongly as the rain ceased when darkness fell.

At the third distance, the 8-hour mark, the order was Miles-Gurney-Rodriguez, with no.5 in eighth place, but Holman & Moody had already lost the Donohue/Hawkins car after a drive-shaft breakage (replaced in 70

Le Mans 24 Hours

minutes) and later gearbox problems. Both Alan Mann entries went out when a suspension upright broke on the Hill/Muir car, and the clutch failed on Gardner and Whitmore's. Just short of 100 laps, after nine hours of racing, the no.6 Holman & Moody car of Andretti and Bianchi blew a head gasket. Four Mk IIs down, four remaining.

Ferrari was having even worse problems; Scarfiotti crashed heavily into wreckage in the Esses and was out on the spot, while Rodriguez had the gearbox fail in the early hours of Sunday. When Bandini's engine broke at 8am, all three factory Ferraris were out, leaving the Ford brigade to race amongst itself, its only competition now the 2-litre factory Porsches, far, far behind. All five privateer GT40s were out.

The Mk IIs had still to make it to 4 pm. Gurney and Miles did not help by starting to race each other, something which Ford race director Leo Beebe immediately called for them to desist. Both cars were running at qualifying pace, turning in 3min 30sec laps, although team orders had set delta times several

- Le Mans rookies Hutcherson (left) and Bucknum know they are in with a chance of the podium after the Ferraris failed, but nothing is being taken for granted. Ronnie gives Dick feedback on conditions before the latter takes over the wheel. *Claude Nahum collection*

- With Hutch aboard 1016, the centralised refuelling system hose is hefted back over the pit wall. Bucknum, foreground, stands by. Most stops were routine, but H&M had to change cracked brake discs six times, and there were also three brake pad changes. *Claude Nahum collection*

seconds slower. Gurney matched his pole position time of 3min 30.6sec.

Then Gurney's leading car holed its radiator and had to make a series of stops for water. As a result, at 9am on Sunday morning, a head gasket blew, and the pole-position car's race was over. Bucknum and Hutcherson had to stop six times, starting at around 9pm Saturday evening, to change the Kelsey-Hayes brake discs after checks revealed cracks, and there were an additional three pad changes. Most of the Mk IIs had to service brakes, but the persistent 1016 stops cost more time than the others.

With three hours to go, Miles and Hulme in the powder blue no.1 (P/1015) had a three-lap lead, but was ordered to allow the no.2 car, the McLaren/Amon black and silver P/1046, to unlap itself; Miles was told to slow on the Mulsanne, and this car's pit stops were lengthened until the two cars were running

1016 goes light as it crests the brow under the Dunlop bridge before sweeping down into the Esses, Hutcherson on board. The NASCAR star had little trouble coming to terms with the French road circuit after years of racing on oval speedways.
Claude Nahum collection

Le Mans 24 Hours

together on the same lead lap.

The drama was not yet over, as the rain returned in the early afternoon, slowing the pace, and the two lead Fords circulated together, closely joined by the Bucknum/Hutcherson car, 1016, a solid third, nine laps ahead of the best of six 2-litre Porsche 906s.

Leo Beebe had ordered the two leaders to finish side-by-side but, just before the finishing line, McLaren accelerated and took the chequered flag a car's length ahead of fellow Kiwi Hulme. Had there been the dead-heat that Beebe wanted, the ACO would have dictated that as the no.2 car had started six metres further back, it had travelled the further distance, and would still be the winner.

Ronnie Bucknum had a grandstand view of the finish from 1016 which was just a few yards behind. Even if it was not a dead heat, the picture of the three Fords taking the flag together would be transmitted across the world.

A year earlier, Ford had been routed by Ferrari, which had scored a 1-2-3 finish while the Blue Oval had failed to get a single car home. Now the tables had been neatly turned – a Ford 1-2-3 with no factory Ferrari making the finish. And the Gurney/Grant Mk II set a new lap record, at an average speed of 142.98mph.

In addition to the Le Mans victory, Ford claimed the 1966 Marques Triple Crown of wins at Daytona, Sebring and now Le Mans, and had won the new 1966 FIA Manufacturers' Prototype Championship from Ferrari by just two points.

One man less than happy with the result was Ken Miles, who had put so much into getting Ford to this point, only for team orders to deny him the triple crown

● This overhead image of three Ford Mk IIs approaching the 1966 finish sees McLaren and Miles still abreast, with Bucknum following, as Ford's Leo Beebe attempts to stage a dead-heat despite the ACO insisting that it would not be accepted.
The Klemantaski Collection/ Yves Debraine

of wins. Yet he was magnanimous about Ford's call – 'They're running the cars, it's their money. They're paying the piper, they can call the tune' – although inwardly, said friends, he was seething.

1016 had played its part to perfection. In total, the no.5 car made 16 pit-stops during the 24 hours, with 10 driver changes, Bucknum running 191 laps in total, to Hutcherson's 157.

Bucknum's longest stint had been 59 laps (60 consecutive laps per driver were the maximum permitted by regulations), from taking the start until handing over the car just before the four-hour mark. His shortest was the final 11 laps to the chequered flag. Hutch's longest run was 50 laps in the early hours of Sunday morning; his shortest was 20 laps between 2pm and 3.10pm.

Despite its braking issues, the car had run strongly, and after the race its true role was revealed in a congratulatory letter to John Holman from Don Frey: 'Your strong third place finish at Le Mans, breaking

At the last moment, McLaren accelerated, denying Miles the chance of the Triple Crown of Daytona, Sebring and Le Mans. Even had they finished level, McLaren was deemed to have travelled the further distance, starting 6 metres behind Miles.
Sutton Images

Le Mans 24 Hours

Chris Amon rides on the winning car (Mk II 1046) driven by Bruce McLaren on its return to the finish area, with 1016 following along behind.
Sutton Images

Don Frey's letter to John Holman a week after Le Mans confirmed that 1016 had been held back in reserve, acknowledging that Bucknum and Hutcherson might just as easily have won as the Shelby American drivers.

all records for a first-time entry, was all the more remarkable in view of the fact that we requested you to hold your car in reserve. We know your car and drivers very well could have won the race, and were deprived of the opportunity only by our instructions, which you followed. Thank you for a superb job.'

Ford's whole ethos of racing at Le Mans was to sell cars, and no time was wasted in putting its formidable marketing operation into action. Once back in America, 1016 was drafted into promotional duties. In the hands of Shelby GT350 builder Bernie Kretzschmar, who had also crewed the Miles/Hulme car at Le Mans, it was collected from Charlotte and started a tour of Ford dealerships across the south-eastern states which lasted until the end of the year.

1966 Le Mans 24 Hours 18-19 June
Round 7 International Manufacturers' Championship

1	Bruce McLaren (NZ)/Chris Amon (NZ)	Ford MK II (1046)	360 laps
2	Ken Miles (GB)/Denny Hulme (NZ)	Ford Mk II (1015)	360 laps
3	**Ronnie Bucknum (USA)/Dick Hutcherson (USA)**	**Ford Mk II (1016)**	**348 laps**
4	Jo Siffert (CH)/Colin Davis (GB)	Porsche 906LE	339 laps
5	Hans Herrmann (D)/Herbert Linge (D)	Porsche 906LE	338 laps
6	Udo Schütz (D)/Peter de Klerk (ZA)	Porsche 906LE	337 laps
7	Guenther Klass (D) Rolf Stommelen (D)	Porsche 906	330 laps
8	Piers Courage (GB)/Roy Pike (USA)	Ferrari 275GTB/C	313 laps
9	Henri Grandsire (F)/Leo Cella (I)	Alpine Renault A210	311 laps
10	Pierre Noblet (F)/Claude Dubois (B)	Ferrari 275GTB/C	319 laps

Dick Hutcherson

Iowa native Dick Hutcherson was a successful stock car racer, winning 12 NASCAR races for Holman & Moody's Ford team in 103 starts between 1965 and 1967. He had already been two-times champion in the mid-west IMCA (International Motorsport Contest Association) championship running stock cars, when John Holman saw his talent and signed him.

He was second in his first full NASCAR season in 1965, but in 1966 Ford withdrew in protest at Chrysler's powerful Hemi engine being re-admitted after a one-year ban on safety grounds, leaving Hutch without a drive.

After Walt Hansgen was killed at the April Le Mans test weekend, and aware of their familiarity with the 7-litre V8, Holman & Moody drafted Hutch and fellow Ford NASCAR racer Marvin Panch into the Ford squad as potential drivers for its 1966 Le Mans 24 Hours campaign. They tried the Mk II at the Kingman high-speed proving ground, but both found it difficult to adjust to the handling of a mid-engined car.

Even so, Hutcherson, 34, was the quicker of the two, and was named as reserve. Then when AJ Foyt suffered burns in an Indycar crash at the Milwaukee Mile in May, Hutch subbed for AJ in the no.5 Mk II, and extensively tested 1016 at Riverside, just three weeks before Le Mans. After taking third place with Ronnie Bucknum in the Le Mans 24 Hours to complete Ford's podium sweep, he returned to NASCAR to take two wins before the end of the season.

In 1967, Plymouth's Richard Petty was the man to beat, and overshadowed the opposition, winning 27 of 44 starts. Hutcherson won two races to place third overall in the standings, but at that point decided to hang up his helmet and become the crew-chief for his friend David Pearson; together they won the 1968 and 1969 NASCAR titles. Then Hutch had a two-year tenure as general manager for Holman & Moody, before setting up his own chassis race shop with Eddie Pagan in 1972.

That was not the end of his driving career, however; in 1976 he was persuaded to share a 7-litre NASCAR Ford Torino at Le Mans, of all places. One of two lumbering American oval cars entered, it had plenty of power, but poor brakes – nonetheless, it lasted until the early hours of Sunday morning when the gearbox failed.

Dick Hutcherson died at age of 73 in 2005, but the Hutcherson-Pagan racing parts company lives on.

● A giant in NASCAR racing, Dick Hutcherson effortlessly made the switch to Le Mans. But after his 1966 podium, it was back to NASCAR. Despite winning races against Richard Petty, he retired from driving to prepare championship-winning Fords in 1968. *The Revs Institute for Automobile Research/Albert Bochroch*

Chapter 9
Daytona 24 Hours
4-5 February 1967

Kar Kraft had been working on a new Ford GT since late 1965. It had an aluminium honeycomb chassis that was half the weight, but just as rigid, as the steel one. The chassis was designed by Ed Hull, with the body design entrusted to Holmer LaGassey Jr by Ford styling chief Gene Bordinat. The brief was to produce a shape capable of 250mph, and although it had the same wheelbase as the GT40, it was narrower - and lower, at 38.5in. The new car - first named the GT-P, but then the J-Car – would still use the 427, and an automatic transmission replacing the heavy T-44 manual. It weighed 226 kg less than the Mk II.

J-1 ran at Le Mans Test Weekend in 1966 – and proved 1.6 seconds a lap quicker than the fastest Mark II - but it broke during testing at Sebring and Ford decided to concentrate on the Mk IIs for that year's Le Mans, rather than risk an unproven car.

But with that Ferrari-beating 1-2-3 in the bag, attention turned back to the lightweight J-1, and a second car, J-2, was built to race in the new Group 7 CanAm series. It was this one which Shelby's development driver Ken Miles was testing at Riverside in August, hitting 180mph on the back stretch before flipping end-over-end, throwing him to his death.

Despite this tragedy, Ford pushed ahead with a third J-car in Group 6 trim with an eye on Daytona, Sebring and Le Mans for 1967. With the modified Mk IIs (later to be called Mk11B) now ready, the decision was taken to run the two types (which shared the same drivetrains) back-to-back at Daytona in December 1966, a week after Ferrari had run at the same track.

Over the winter, Shelby and Holman & Moody had been retained to develop what would become the Mk IIB – although it was not called that officially until Le Mans. Improvements included bigger rear Halibrand 'turbine-style' wheels, reshaped wings front and rear, a lighter front panel, a shorter rear deck (now without the brake snorkels), glass-fibre seats, an aluminium dashboard, and other weight savings.

The Mk IIBs were strong, although slower than the two Ferrari P4s, but J-3 proved a handful on the banking and eventually broke a suspension pick-up point, damaging the chassis. The decision was taken to stick to the Mk IIBs for the 1967 Daytona 24 Hours.

Drawing on its NASCAR experience, Holman & Moody designed an advanced fire extinguisher system, and fitted roll cages. These put 55kg back on, but were considered a worthwhile trade-off for driver safety. The investment was to prove its worth when Peter Revson crashed his Mk IIB at 160mph at a later Daytona test, walking away from a series of end-over-end somersaults.

A major test at Riverside had again thrown up concerns about the T-34 automatic transmission, all the drivers preferring the heavier but reliable T-44 manual. Girling brakes were finally replaced for good with huge iron Kelsey-Hayes discs, and Holman & Moody modified the calipers to speed-up disc changes.

Ford also decided to revert to cast-iron cylinder heads with two 4-barrel Holley 652 CFM carburettors, with tunnel-port, over-and-under inlet manifolds. In this form, the 427 produced an extra 45bhp, but at a cost of another 23kg.

1016 was up-dated to this specification when it

Still in gold, 1016 has its last race as a factory car at the 1967 Daytona 24 Hours, now upgraded to what will eventually be called the Mk IIB; it was once again used as a test mule for improvements, while the Mk IV was developed. *The Revs Institute for Automobile Research/Eric della Faille*

Daytona 24 Hours

● A youthful Mark Donohue posing with 1016 in the makeshift Daytona pits, was teamed for the 1967 24 Hours with another rising American star, Peter Revson. Note the Mercury stripe, promoting Ford's up-market sales division.
The Revs Institute for Automobile Research/ Albert Bochroch

returned from its promotional tour, in time to join the squad for Daytona. It was one of six Mk IIBs entered, shared between Shelby and Holman & Moody, faced against three factory Ferrari P4s and two Chaparral 2Fs.

Still coloured gold, but now with thin black stripes atop the body and black side flashes promoting Ford's Mercury division, 1016 ran as no.4, to be driven by Mark Donohue and Peter Revson, the New York cosmetic company heir who was starting to make his name in US racing. It qualified 12th, four seconds off the pace of pole-sitter Dan Gurney's Shelby car, which was also entered as a Mercury.

The race was a litany of transmission and suspension disasters. The six Mk IIs got through 11 gearboxes following the same output shaft failures; 1016 had its first change less than four hours into the race, having

Daytona 24 Hours

ENTRIES FOR 1967 DAYTONA 24-HOUR CONTINENTAL

No.	Type Car	Class	CC'S	Year	Entrant	Drivers
1	Ford GT Mark II	Proto	7010	1966	Ford Motor Co. (SA), Dearborn, Mich.	A. J. Foyt, Houston, Texas; Dan Gurney, Santa Ana, Calif.
2	Ford GT Mark II	Proto	7010	1966	Ford Motor Co. (SA), Dearborn, Mich.	Ronnie Bucknum, Palaya del Rey, Calif.; Frank Gardner, Palm Beach Sydney, Australia
3	Ford GT Mark II	Proto	7010	1966	Ford Motor Co. (SA), Dearborn, Mich.	Bruce McLaren, Colnbrook, England; Lucien Bianchi, Brussels, Belgium
4	Ford GT Mark II	Proto	7000	1967	Ford Motor Co. (HM), Dearborn, Mich.	Mark Donohue, Stony Brook, N.Y.; Peter Revson, New York City, N.Y.
5	Ford GT Mark II	Proto	7000	1967	Ford Motor Co. (HM), Dearborn, Mich.	Paul Hawkins, Sydney, Australia; Lloyd Ruby, Wichita Falls, Texas; Dennis Hulme, New Zealand
6	Ford GT Mark II	Proto	7000	1967	Ford Motor Co. (HM), Dearborn, Mich.	Skip Scott, Devon, Pa.; Mario Andretti, Nazareth, Pa.; Richie Ginther, Granda Hills, Calif.
7	S. A. Cobra	Sports	7010	1966	Herb W. Byrne, Cape Canaveral, Fla.	Herb Byrne, Cape Canaveral, Fla.; Dick Thetford, Cape Canaveral, Fla.; Russel Beazell, Fort Myers, Fla.
8	Corvette Gran Sport	Proto	7000	1964	Jim White Chevrolet Inc., Toledo, Ohio	Al Denman, Fremont, Ohio; Bobby Brown, Long Island, N.Y.
9	Ford GT 40	Sports	4736	1967	Brescia Racine Corse, Brescia, Italy	Umberto Maglioli, Italy; Mario Casoni, Italy
11	Ford GT 40	Sports	4736	1966	J. W. Engineering (GD), London, England	Dr. Richard Thompson, Alexandria, Va.; Jackie Ickx, Braine-l'Allerd, Belgium
14	Chaparral (2-D)	Proto	4999	1966	Chaparral Cars, Inc., Midland, Texas	Bob Johnson, Columbus, Ohio; Bruce Jennings, Towson, Md.
15	Chaparral (2F)	Proto	4999	1967	Chaparral Cars, Inc., Midland, Texas	Phil Hill, Santa Monica, Calif.; Mike Spence, Birkshire, England
16	Chevrolet Camero	Touring	4952	1967	Joie Chitwood, Sr., Tampa, Fla.	Joie Chitwood, Jr., Tampa, Fla.; Jack McClure, Tampa, Fla.
17	Ford Falcon	Touring	4727	1964	Bob Johnson, Columbus, Ohio	Tom Payne, Birmingham, Mich.; Don S_____, Lancaster, Ohio
18	Shelby GT 350	GT	4727	1966	Roger West, Birmingham, Ala.	Roger ___, Bobby ___
19	Ford Falcon	Touring	4727	1964	Howmet Corp., Conshohocken, Penna.	Ray B___
20	Ford GT 40	Sports	4700	1966	William Wonder, Inc., Locust Valley, N.Y.	Willia___, Raym___
21	Dodge Dart	Touring	4600	1966	Brock Yates, Castile, N.Y.	Brock ___, Charl___
22	Plymouth Barracuda	Touring	4482	1967	JoKar Racing Associates, Nashua, N.H.	Frank ___, Raym___
23	Ferrari P4	Proto	4000	1967	Ferrari s.p.a., Modena, Italy	Loren___, Chris___
24	Ferrari P4	Proto	4000	1967	Ferrari s.p.a., Modena, Italy	Ludo___, Mike___
25	Ferrari Dino	Proto	2000	1967	Scuderia Sant Ambroeus srl., Milan, Italy	Bisce___
26	Ferrari P4	Proto	4000	1967	N. American Racing Team, New York City	Pedr___, Jean___
27	Ferrari P3	Proto	3285	1966	North American Racing Team, New York City, New York	Pete___, Jo S___
29	Ferrari GTB	GT	3285	1966	Pedro Rodriguez, Jr., Mexico City, Mexico	Carl___, Hec___
31	Ferrari P3	Proto	3285	1966	David Piper, London, England	Dav___, Ric___
32	Ferrari 250 LM	Sports	3285	1965	Peter Clarke, London, England	Pete___
33	Ferrari 275 LM RP4	Proto	3285	1965	Ecurie Francorchamps, Brussels, Belgium	Wil___
35	Ferrari Dino	Proto	1987	1967	Modern Classic Motors, Reno, Nevada	Ch___, Bu___
36	Chevrolet Camero	Touring	5000	1967	Roger Penske, Gladwyne, P.	Ge___, Jo___
40	Camero	Touring	4952	1967	Craig Fisher, Toronto, Canada	Cr___, Ge___
42	Triumph TR4A	GT	2186	1967	Cannons Auto Service, Daytona Beach, Fla.	St___, G___
43	Triumph TR4A	GT	2186	1966	Cannons Auto Service, Daytona Beach, Fla.	D___, A___
44	Triumph TR4A	GT	2138	1964	Raymond Stoutenburg, Manteo, N.C.	R___, J___, R___

● The official entry (left), and Ford's report on the race (below) showing a catalogue of disasters. The race was Ford's to win, but a transmission manufacturing error saw every Mk II suffer, all requiring gearbox changes, and only one finished.

DAYTONA CONTINENTAL 24-HOUR RACE — Feb. 4-5, 1967

CAR NO./ DRIVER	AV. LAP SPEED	FUEL CONS. (M/G)	OIL CONS. (M/Q)	TIRE WEAR (Laps)	PAD WEAR (Laps)	PROBLEMS
#1 McLaren/Bianchi	2:06-2:07	4.0	150	220 F / 120 R	200 F / 340 R	Gear box change at 245 laps (8.5 hrs.). Water system pressurizing after 57 laps, water added every 15-20 laps thereafter, maximum possible rpm was 5500 with 1/2 to 3/4 throttle to avoid overheating. Vehicle completed 593 laps to finish 7th.
#2 Bucknum/Gardner	2:01-2:02	4.7	200	220 F / 120 R	200 F / 340 R	Gear box changed first half-hour, second gear box at 274 laps (10.5 hours). Vehicle retired after 274 laps (11 hours) due to lack of gear boxes.
#3 Foyt/Gurney	1:58-1:59	4.7	200	200 F / 120 R	180 F / 360 R	Battery changed at 132 laps due to starter relay failure. Gear box failure at 276 laps (9.25 hours). Water system pressurized on lap 148, problem intermittent. Vehicle retired at 464 laps while running in 4th or 5th position with engine failure.
#4 Donahue/Revson	2:02	5.0	175	165 F / 118 R		Left rear shock changed on lap 21. Transmission changed on lap 118. Engine push-rod failure also on lap 118. Transmission failure at 236 laps (approx. 10 hours) and car was retired.
#5 Andretti/Ginther	1:59	5.0	150			Transmission failed at lap 100, second one at Lap 301. Car retired lap 301 (12 hours).
#6 Ruby/Hulme	2:01	4.8	164	150 F / 100 R		Transmission failed at lap 193, starter ring gear failed at 210 laps, engine push-rod failure at 280 laps. Car was retired at 301 laps (12 hours).

** All figures at this time are approximate.

Daytona 24 Hours

● 1016 on the Daytona infield course, about to turn onto the South Banking; after one transmission change after four hours, it retired when a second failed at 10 hours; the six Mk IIs had used 11 gearboxes and there were none left.
Claude Nahum collection

two hours earlier had a shock-absorber change. No. 4's crew chief Jimmy Tucker, and his two assistants Richie Barsz and Norman Lockwood, certainly earned their money that weekend, but 1016 finally retired at 10 hours as there were no further transmissions available. No-one knew it at the time, but this had been its last world championship race.

Only one Ford finished, that of Bruce McLaren and Lucien Bianchi, which had two gearbox changes as well as a leaking head gasket. Overheating badly, it somehow smoked and misfired round to complete the 24 hours in seventh place. The factory Ferraris finished an untroubled 1-2-3 - sweet revenge for the previous June - and had generally been faster. Now the question was: what did the Mk II have left to give?

Writing of the Daytona disaster, John Wanderer said,

'It was evident that a little refinement will be necessary in the pit work. This situation will be relieved by experience on the part of the crew, and a lessening of a parts-changing panic which is like a disease and creates more confusion. It is felt that no comment on the outcome of the race is necessary.' That last line referred to the output shaft failures between 3rd and 4th gears, which a post-mortem identified as having been down to faulty heat-treatment by an outside supplier.

Daytona was an utter rout for Ford, and one which would have immediate repercussions. The Mk IIBs had been outpaced by both Ferrari and Chaparrral, and Roy Lunn was now pushing for the J-Car to be brought in as Ford's principal weapon. Lunn had at least one ally at Shelby in Phil Remington, who believed that the car had potential if its aerodynamics could be improved,

Daytona 24 Hours

Sweet revenge: the factory Ferrari 330 P4s of Bandini/Amon (No 23) and Parkes/Scarfiotti (No 24) sweep across the Daytona finish line, below them the NART 330 P3 of Rodriguez/Guichet, for a payback 1-2-3 finish. The fourth-placed Porsche rubs it in.
The Revs Institute for Automobile Research/Eric della Faille

something which the December Daytona test had shown was sorely lacking.

So Remington and his best fabricators, Bill Eaton and Dennis Gragg, went to work on J-1 at Dearborn, joined by Ed Hull and three Ford Styling craftsmen. Retaining the original centre section with the doors and screen, they built up a new, sleeker body over a week. When it was rolled into the wind-tunnel, it generated 100lb less drag than the original J-Car, and so the Mk IV was born.

'It was perfect right out of the box', said Shelby crew chief Gordon Chance. 'It was designed and built in the United States, not in England; no Italian gearbox, nothing. At Sebring it was 7-10 seconds faster than Foyt's Mk IIB. I never had a better day in my life.'

> **The Ferraris finished 1-2-3 and had been generally faster. What did the Mk II have left to give?**

1967 Daytona 24 Hours 4-5 February
Round 1 International Manufacturers' Championship

1	Lorenzo Bandini (I)/Chris Amon (NZ)	Ferrari 330P4	666 laps
2	Mike Parkes (GB)/Ludovico Scarfiotti (I)	Ferrari 330P4	663 laps
3	Pedro Rodriguez (MEX)/Jean Guichet (F)	Ferrari 330P4	637 laps
4	Hans Herrmann (D)/Jo Siffert (CH)	Porsche 910	618 laps
5	Dieter Spoerry (CH)/Rico Steinemann (CH)	Porsche 906LE	608 laps
6	Dick Thompson (USA)/Jacky Ickx (B)	Ford GT40 (1049)	601 laps
7	Bruce McLaren (NZ)/ Lucien Bianchi (B)	Ford Mk II (1012)	593 laps
8	William Wonder (USA)/Raymond Caldwell (USA)	Ford GT40 (103)	573 laps
9	Jack Ryan (USA)/Bill Bencker (USA)	Porsche 911	555 laps
10	George Drolsom (USA) /Harold Williamson (USA)	Porsche 911	542 laps
DNF	**Mark Donohue (USA)/Peter Revson (USA)**	**Ford Mk II (1016)**	**236 laps transmission**

Peter Revson

The heir to the American Revlon cosmetics empire fortune, Peter Revson was born in New York in 1939, and got the taste for racing in a Morgan, whilst still at the University of Hawaii. In 1963, he went to Europe to race in Formula Junior, towing his car behind an old baker's van, before returning to America.

The 1967 Daytona 24 Hours was his only outing in a works Ford. He was teamed with Mark Donohue in 1016 but the car was the first of the Mk IIs to retire, shortly after eight hours. In this race all the Mk IIs suffered the same gearbox failure: a shaft which had been badly heat-treated.

In 1968 Revson finished 12th in the Sebring 12 Hours in a TransAm AMC Javelin with Skip Scott. The following year he continued in TransAm with a Ford Mustang and drove a Brabham-Repco in the Indianapolis 500, finishing fifth. In 1970 he teamed with Steve McQueen, and the pair finished second in the Sebring 12 Hours in the actor's Porsche 908. Further TransAm racing followed with Roger Penske and then Revvie discovered the Can-Am.

As a part of the all-conquering McLaren Can-Am team, he became the first American to win the title in 1971, with five victories. The same year he took pole position at Indy for McLaren, and finished second to Al Unser, with AJ Foyt third. Bruce McLaren had been killed testing at Goodwood in 1970, but his team continued under Teddy Mayer, who recognised Revson's undoubted talent with a place in his Formula 1 team; Revvie responded by winning both the 1973 British and Canadian Grands Prix.

He moved to Don Nichols' new Shadow team for 1974, with which he took sixth place in the non-championship Brands Hatch Race of Champions. Five days later he was testing at Kyalami for the South African Grand Prix, when his car had a front suspension ball-joint failure and crashed under safety barriers, killing him instantly. He was just 35 years old.

- Peter Revson may have been an heir to the Revlon empire, but he learned his craft the hard way, trailing his formula car around Europe. After his only race with Ford at Daytona, he joined McLaren in F1, winning in Britain and Canada.
The Revs Institute for Automobile Research/ Duke Q Manor & Max Le Grand

- Revson's biggest success was in Can-Am, where he was 1971 champion after five wins with the mighty McLaren M8F-Chevrolet. The same year he finished 2nd in the Indy 500 after putting his McLaren on pole.
The Revs Institute for Automobile Research/Albert Bochroch

Mark Donohue

New Jersey-born Mark Donohue had a rare talent among race drivers: the ability to not only score multiple victories, but also to prepare and set up his cars. Armed with a degree in engineering, this talent quickly showed when he won his first-ever event, a hill-climb, and went on to take a 1961 SCCA championship driving an Elva Courier.

He was soon spotted by veteran racer Walt Hansgen, whose Ferrari 275GTB he shared in the 1965 Sebring 12 Hours, finishing 12th. That same year, Donohue took SCCA race wins in a Shelby GT350 and a Formule Libre Lotus 20 single-seater.

During two years working in New York on the development of the TVR Griffith (a 4.7-litre V8 version of the British TVR Grantura), he also raced Jack Griffith's Shelby Cobra with much success. At Hansgen's suggestion, Ford signed 29-year old Donohue for its 1966 Le Mans campaign, and he joined Hansgen at Holman & Moody.

They formed a great partnership at the wheel of the new Ford Mk II, finishing third in the Daytona 24 Hours, and third in the Sebring 12 Hours. Their next race would have been Le Mans, but at the April Test Weekend two weeks after Sebring, 46-year old Hansgen died after crashing into a pile of sand blocking an escape road.

Donohue put the loss of his mentor behind him to share with Australian Paul Hawkins, but they posted the first Ford retirement after a drive-shaft breakage. They were out after just 12 laps, as three of the sister cars went on to take the 1-2-3 finish.

'Captain Nice' – as Donohue was widely known – was called back by Ford for 1967, when he shared 1016 with Peter Revson in the Daytona 24 Hours, but along with five of the six Mk IIs entered, retired with gearbox failure. At Le Mans he drove a Mk IV with Bruce McLaren. The pair, both brilliant engineers, could never agree on chassis set-up, but McLaren put the canary yellow car on pole, and they brought it home fourth, despite being delayed by the engine cover blowing off.

The previous year, race team owner Roger Penske had spoken to Donohue at Hansgen's funeral, and in 1967 they formed what would become one of the most

Le Mans Test Weekend

driving) was able to provide a mass of comparison statistics; 1016 was on Firestone tyres, the Mk IV on Goodyear, yet both ran the same 202.70 mph maximum speed on the Mulsanne straight. Ford had its own speed traps, and noted that the best Ferrari could do was 191.5mph.

Donohue ended the test as fourth fastest with an official lap time of 3min 32.6sec, three seconds better than McLaren who was fifth fastest, although Ford was quick to point out that both cars were there to gather data, and not to set fastest times.

Nonetheless, 1016 had shown that a well-sorted Mk IIB was still as competitive as the new kid on the block; granted, it was 34kg lighter than the Mk IV, and its uprated engine was producing 50bhp more than the 427 in the Mk IV, but it was a high note on which to exit.

1016 was flown to New York on 11 April, then trucked back to Charlotte, where Ford decided not to race it at Le Mans, but to retire it with honour.

Once back at Holman & Moody, it was cleaned up. A memo from Wanderer to Ford FVA's Homer Perry on 3 August 1967 had noted that, '1016 requires an engine, paint job, rear structure, and other minor components'. Accordingly, another engine was installed and it officially became a show car.

1967 Le Mans 24 Hours Tests 8-9 April

1	Lorenzo Bandini (I) Ferrari 330 P4	3m 25.5s
2	Mike Parkes (GB) Ferrari 330P4	3m 27.6s
3	John Surtees (GB) Lola-Aston Martin T70 Mk3	3m 31.9s
4	**Mark Donohue (USA) Ford Mk IIB (1016)**	**3m 32.6s**
5	Bruce McLaren (NZ) Ford Mk IV (J-3)	3m 35.6s

● In pre-telemetry days, data was collected through wired sensors which fed into bulky equipment in the nose of the car and in the passenger well. Engineers could read speeds, braking effect, and suspension behaviour (see graph right) around every lap.
LAT Images

Le Mans Test Weekend

In the days before wi-fi, when an IBM computer filled a room, data-logging was a nascent science. This was Donohue's last drive for Ford, and 1016's last appearance as a factory car; it did not compete at Le Mans in 1967.
Claude Nahum collection

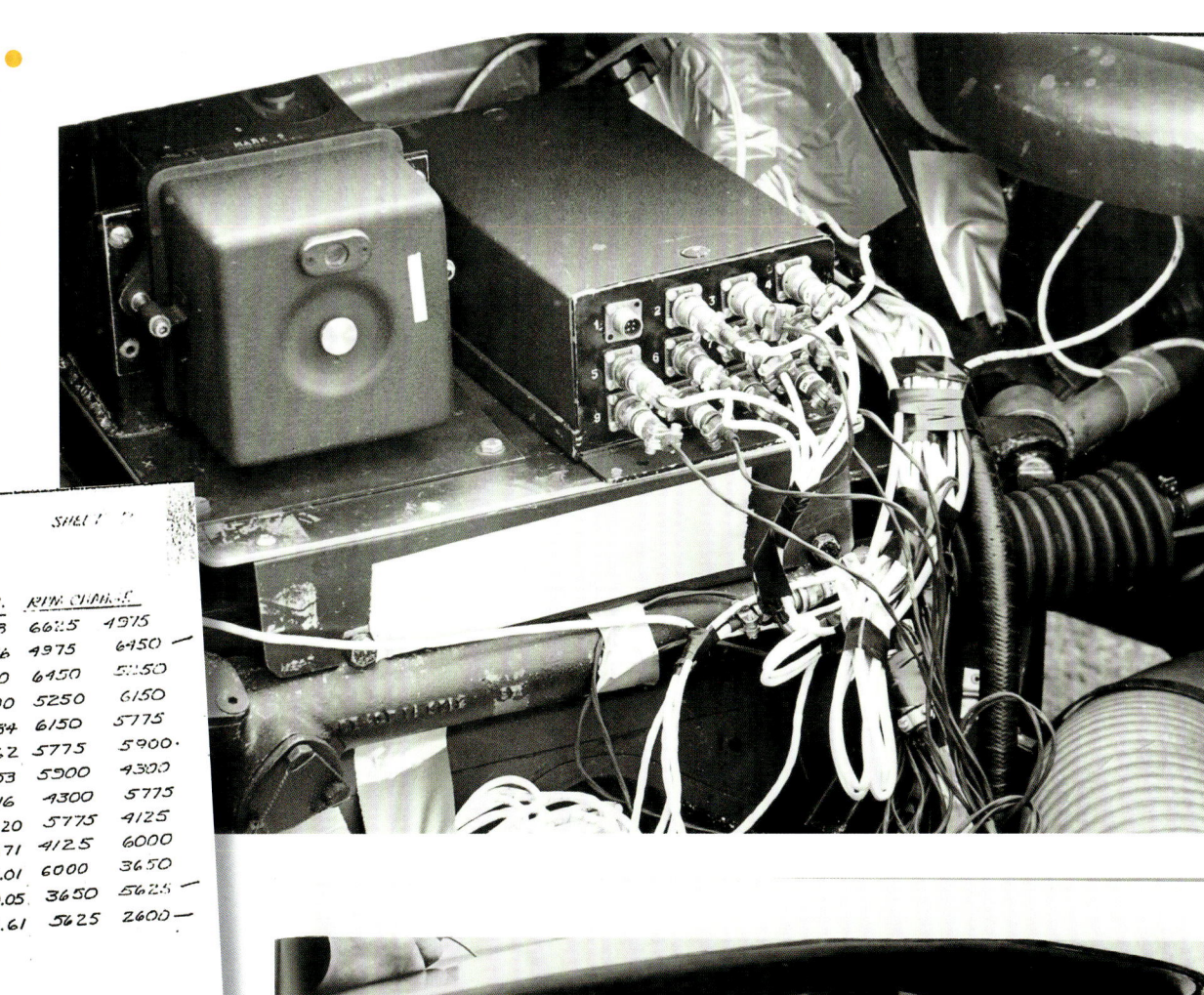

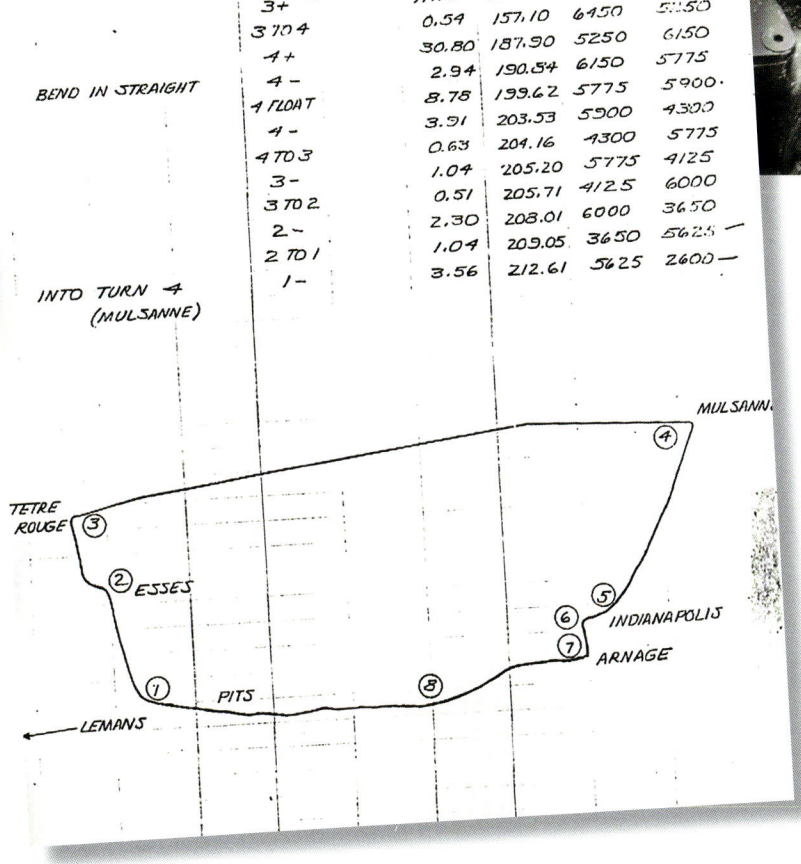

Ford GT40 MkII 1016

Chapter 11
Postscript to 1967

The Mk IV would spearhead Ford's last effort at Le Mans and the defence of its 1966 title. 1016 was not destined to be among the four Mk IVs and four Mk IIBs being readied for the French race. The cars were shared between Shelby and Holman & Moody, hedging their bets that one or other of the types should win. They were backed up by a further three privateer GT40s, one run by John Wyer, one by Ford France, and one by Filipinetti.

Ford's 1967 Le Mans assault was described by Preston Lerner as 'less like a race team than an expeditionary force assembled to establish a beachhead in enemy territory'. In total, there were 125 people, including 14 drivers, 24 mechanics, and all the support crews and Ford executives.

Among further improvements which had been made to the 7-litre V8 was a reversion to alloy heads to save weight, and power was boosted to 500bhp at 6,400rpm (a 15bhp increase on 1966) by a bigger pair of four-barrel Holleys and a dual-plane intake manifold. Dyno tests showed the upgraded engine could run up to 48 hours without any drama.

Bruce McLaren put his Holman & Moody Mk IV on pole, beating Mike Spence's Chaparral, with the Andretti/Bianchi Shelby Mk IV third on the grid. Then it was all Ford back to the best Ferrari, the Parkes/Scarfiotti 330 P4 in seventh place.

Dan Gurney had finished Le Mans only once in nine starts, but he had a gut feeling this was to be his year. He was sharing the red Mk IV with AJ Foyt, who was fresh from winning the Indianapolis 500, but had never even seen Le Circuit de la Sarthe until race week. From the start, Gurney played a waiting game, looking after the brakes and letting the race come to him.

Both Chaparrals retired before mid-distance, and then the Fords went out one by one, two with engine failures and one catching fire, severely burning Mike Salmon. Lloyd Ruby crashed his Holman & Moody Mk IV after sliding off on oil dropped at Tertre Rouge shortly after 9pm. Worse was to come: at 3.30 Sunday morning, Mario Andretti left the pits in his Holman & Moody Mk IV after a pad change, and arrived at the Esses to find himself brakeless – he had failed to bed-in the pads – and crashed into the bank. As he climbed out of his wrecked car, badly bruised by the seat belts, Roger McCluskey piled his Mk IIB into the wall in avoidance, only to be collected by the Ford France/Holman & Moody Mk IIB of Jo Schlesser. All four Holman & Moody cars were out, leaving Ford with just two Shelby Mk IVs still running. Fortunately for the Blue Oval, those two cars were in first and fourth places.

Then, soon after dawn, McLaren had his car's tail section blow off on the Mulsanne straight; with no spare available, the team sent him out again to find it and he drove back holding it in place with one hand through the open driver's door. A further 48 minutes were lost in repairs, but he and Donohue finished in fourth place behind the other Ford and two Ferraris, albeit 29 laps down on the leader.

Gurney and Foyt had run further and faster than any car in the long history of Le Mans, covering 3,251.57 miles at an average speed of 135.48mph, pit-stops included. On the podium, the Californian shook the magnum of champagne and sprayed the crowd,

The J-car had become the Mk IV, four of which were entered for Le Mans 1967, along with four Mk IIBs. While they shared wheelbase and drivetrains, they were structurally and aerodynamically worlds apart.
Ford

Postscript to 1967

- Beauty is in the eye of the beholder, but there is no denying that the Mk IV was aesthetically perfect. Gurney and Foyt took 'Red 1' to Le Mans victory over the factory Ferraris, running faster and further than any car before.
The Revs Institute for Automotive Research/Eric della Faille

starting a new trend that has continued through the years since.

Recalling the celebration, some years later, Gurney said: 'I never thought about it at the time. Hank the Deuce was there with his new bride, I think on their honeymoon, when I started spraying him. I'm not sure if he liked it or not, but he was a good sport about it, and AJ and I had a wonderful time spraying champagne. It seemed the right way to finish a perfect weekend.'

It was the first and only all-American victory at Le Mans: an all-American car, prepared by an American team and driven by American drivers. Brute force had beaten Italian sophistication for the second time, and two more Ford victories (from John Wyer's Gulf team) would follow in 1968 and 1969. Only Ferrari or Ford won the Le Mans 24 Hours throughout the Sixties.

But neither Gurney nor Foyt were to race at

Le Mans again – and nor were Ford USA, Shelby, or Holman & Moody, at least not in the prototype category. It was not until 2016, 50 years after that 1-2-3, that Ford returned as a factory team with the new Ford GTs in the capable hands of Chip Ganassi Racing. They won first time out, albeit in the LM GTE class rather than outright.

Ford's investment in the GT40 Le Mans programme over its five years totalled $22 million. Don Frey had told John Wyer after the 1966 race, 'I know it's possible to win this race for less than $7 million, but there seems no way Ford can do it.'

During the four years, 1964-67, that it ran a factory programme, Ford had entered 59 GT40s and variants in 17 races and won just six of them. But two of those wins were the Le Mans 24 Hours – and that, from the start, was the main objective.

While Ford wound down its factory effort after the 1967 Le Mans win, John Wyer had been waiting in the wings with his Gulf-sponsored 5 litre Gulf GT40 Mk 1s, and Rodriguez/Bianchi won in 1968. Wyer said Ford could have done it three years earlier had they listened…
Ford

JW Gulf won again in 1969, the closest unstaged finish in the history of the race, Jacky Ickx by 100 metres from the Porsche 908 of Hans Herrmann. It was Ford's last Le Mans win; the following year would see the first of 19 outright victories for Porsche.
Ford

Part 3
The Second Life of 1016

● Forty-two years after its final outing as factory car, 1016 is hustled by Claude Nahum around the 2008 Circuit des Remparts d'Angouleme, a French mini-Monaco for historic race cars. It is now back in its 1966 Le Mans livery with rear deck snorkels.
Claude Nahum collection/ICR

When GT40 P/1016 ended its short racing career in the 1960s, it looked as if the car which had helped Ford to win Le Mans would be consigned to history, in the halls of Harrah's Automobile Collection in Reno, Nevada.

Far from it; 15 years after being donated by Ford, 1016 was sold, along with other cars no longer wanted. Once the small matter of its being mistakenly identified as the car which finished second in the 1966 Le Mans 24 Hours had been resolved, it started a new life as an historic racer and show car, a revival which continues to this day.

After a string of post-1983 owners, and a total rebuild by its original race team Holman & Moody, 1016 is now in the hands of Turkish entrepreneur and race driver Claude Nahum. Today, despite its 50-plus years, it is probably in far better shape than it was in the 1960s.

Iconic venues such as Watkins Glen, Pebble Beach, Goodwood, Villa d'Este, Le Mans, Chantilly and Road America have all figured in 1016's second life, and it is rarely at home in Claude's Geneva workshops. 1016 is an icon itself, a truly exceptional car.

Chapter 12
Renewed and back on track

On 26 February 1968, Ford Motor Company donated 1016 to Harrah's Automobile Collection in Reno, Nevada, along with the Mk IV driven by Hulme and Ruby at Le Mans in 1967.

In his letter to Harrah's, Ford vice president George de Havilland had mistakenly identified 1016 as P/1015, the second-place car at Le Mans in 1966 (and FoMoCo had even given it a P/1015 identification plate).

1016 was displayed at Harrah's in its 1967 Le Mans Test Weekend trim (gold, with data-logging equipment still on-board), sitting alongside J-8, until 1983, when it was sold to Leslie Barth, from New Haven, Connecticut. Barth, not unreasonably believing it was P/1015, had it repainted in a similar pale blue shade to that of the Miles/Hulme Le Mans car.

Barth was to sell it to Nick Soprano and, in 1988, it passed on to Peter Livanos, the Connecticut-domiciled Greek shipping tycoon, who was later to save Aston Martin with Victor Gauntlett. Livanos commissioned Shelby engineers Carroll Smith and Steele Therkelsen to prepare and run the car in selected historic races, notably the 1989 Watkins Glen 2 Hours, in which invited drivers Jacky Ickx and Brian Redman (famous in GT40 circles for their wins for the JW Gulf team in 1968 and 1969) finished second.

1016 changed hands several more times – Californians Bruce Ziegler and James Mazotta, then Wisconsin restorer and tuner George Stauffer, among later owners – before it was bought in November 1992 by Columbus, Ohio enthusiast Ken Quintenz. After some detective work, Quintenz uncovered 1016's true identity, and commissioned Stauffer Classics to restore it to Le Mans 1966 configuration and trim.

The work, carried out by Jeff Sine, include repairing cracked bodywork, refitting the door bubble, and replacing rear aluminium grilles and surrounds. He also re-fabricated the Holman & Moody rear frame and body supports, and all aluminium parts were re-anodised and then polished to their original finish. Sine was able to confirm to Quintenz that he indeed had the original 1966 body panels – 'the repairs, the pop-rivet holes, the scoops, etc, all match June 1966 photographs', he reported.

The body was refitted before respraying in gold with the dayglo pink patches, and the Halibrand wheels were shot-blasted and repainted with their distinctive green centres and red spinners. 1016 was now largely back to its 1966 Le Mans glory, although some 1967 features remained – the H&M roll-cage, the Mk IIB aluminium instrument panel, the fuel system, the rear-mounted oil tank (moved from above the front bulkhead, where it had baked drivers' feet) and the rear deck scoop grilles.

Work was completed by July 1993, in time for the Shelby American Automobile Club's 18th Convention at Watkins Glen, where the three 1966 Le Mans podium cars were back together for the first time in their winning liveries, making an iconic cover for *Shelby American* magazine. Ken Quintenz, together with his sons Darren and Brian, then embarked on a three-year historic racing programme, mainly at Elkhart Lake and Mid-Ohio. But 45 days before 1016 was due to go to Europe for Ford's 30th Anniversary gathering at Le Mans in 1996, Ken crashed heavily at Elkhart Lake.

Claude Nahum has been a regular at the Le Mans Classic since becoming the owner of 1016 in 2004; this is at the 2008 edition, riding the kerbs through (fittingly) the Ford chicane.
Claude Nahum collection

Renewed and back on track

Ford Motor Company,

OFFICE OF THE VICE PRESIDENT
PRODUCT PLANNING AND STYLING

P. O. BOX 2110
DEARBORN, MICHIGAN

February 26, 1968

Mr. William P. Harrah
Harrah's Automobile Collection
P. O. Box 10
Reno, Nevada 89501

Dear Mr. Harrah:

On behalf of the Ford Motor Company I am pleased to confirm the gift of two of our most successful and important GT40 race cars to your outstanding collection. They are:

1. 1966 Ford GT40 Mark II serial 1015. It was the number 1 car driven by Ken Miles and Denis Hulme to second overall at the 1966 Le Mans 24-Hour Race.

2. 1967 Ford GT40 Mark IV serial J-8 driven at Le Mans in 1967 by Lloyd Ruby and Denis Hulme.

Both vehicles are currently at the Holman and Moody shop in Charlotte, N.C. to be refurbished before presentation to your collection. As the work nears completion we will be in contact to finalize the transfer ceremony.

I look forward to seeing them on display on my next visit to your facility.

Sincerely,

George A. Haviland

GAG/aeg

● The letter which caused confusion: Ford VP George de Havilland mistakenly identified 1016 as 1015 when the car was donated to Harrah's Automobile Collection in Nevada. It was not until 1993 that its true identity was revealed by Ken Quintenz.

Exceptional Cars

Renewed and back on track

Lee Holman (son of John) and his English H&M colleague Jim Rose quickly repaired the cosmetic damage, but a rebuild would be needed after the trip. Ken was able to run slow laps at Le Mans and at the Goodwood Festival of Speed the following month, before sending 1016 back to Charlotte (for the first time in 29 years) for a total restoration.

There, Rose and fellow H&M crewman Jimmy Tucker completely restored the chassis, engine, and transaxle, replaced the side pontoons, fabricated new body panels, and made a replacement nose. The restoration bill, presented in March 1997, was for more than $135,000, but worth every cent.

'We also replaced the fuel cell skins which had rusted, and repaired all the crash damage,' recalled Lee Holman. 'We put the chassis back in the original jig (which H&M had shipped over after JWAE closed down), so it was now as new, all the suspension pick-up points correctly aligned. Ken was happy – until then, he had never completed a race or enjoyed the car. Now he started winning, and didn't miss a lap.'

Still gold, 1016 sat in Harrah's for 15 years with its 1967 Le Mans test weekend No 2 on the door, next to the No 4 Mk IV of Hulme/Ruby, which crashed out of the 1967 race when Ruby came across oil.
Claude Nahum collection

When Leslie Barth acquired what he believed to be the 1966 Le Mans second-placed car in 1983, he had it put into the powder-blue livery of the Hulme/Miles car. It was raced at Watkins Glen in 1989 by Jacky Ickx and Brian Redman (centre, behind car).
Claude Nahum collection

Ford GT40 MkII 1016

Renewed and back on track

The Quintenz family continued to use 1016 for regular competition, its biggest success a win at the Shelby Reunion Zippo US Vintage Grand Prix at The Glen in September 2001. It was noted at the time that a Holman & Moody car had beaten two Shelby cars, a neat reversal of 1966…

In 2001, it went to Dearborn for Ford's Racing Centennial, rejoining its 1966 podium colleagues, and in 2003 was back there again for Ford Motor Company's Centennial. The same year, 1016 appeared at the Goodwood Festival of Speed, where Ford's 1966 1-2-3 was the central display – and a replica was part of the sculpture that loomed over Goodwood House. Back in the States in August, 1016 won the prestigious People's Choice Award at the Pebble Beach Concours.

But after 12 years with the Quintenz family, the time had come for 1016 to move on. It was bought through Symbolic Motorcars by Claude Nahum, a Turkish entrepreneur, engineer and race car collector based in Geneva. Nahum had the car inspected by experts prior to purchase in March 2004. Their report noted: 'Externally it is in 1966 Le Mans configuration, with the

- Ken Quintenz bought 1016 in 1992, and after some detective work realised its true identity. Stauffer Classics carried out the respray and a partial restoration, confirming from contemporary photographs that it was indeed the 1966 bodywork, *Claude Nahum collection*

- The car was returned to its 1966 Le Mans 24 Hours livery in time for the 1993 Shelby Convention at Watkins Glen. It was the first time that the three winning cars had been reunited in 27 years, *Claude Nahum collection*

Renewed and back on track

● After crashing at Elkhart Lake just weeks before the 1996 30th Anniversary Reunion at Le Mans, 1016 underwent a total restoration at Holman & Moody, using the original GT40 chassis jigs which had been acquired when JWAE closed.
Holman & Moody

Renewed and back on track

● A few busy seasons of historic racing meant 1016 was scheduled for a further rebuild at Holman & Moody in 2000. Removing the massive 7 litre V8 engine shows just what a tight fit it was in the Mk II.
Holman & Moody

Renewed and back on track

Ken Quintenz and his sons enjoyed considerable success with 1016. This was Ken's finest hour – a win in the Zippo US Vintage Grand Prix at Watkins Glen in 2001. *Claude Nahum collection/ Steve Rossini*

exception of a 1967 Mk IIB passenger door. Otherwise it is extremely original.' The updated passenger door was required to clear the bulky Mk IIB roll-cage installed in all cars for the 1967 season.

Nahum paid $2.4 million for 1016, and it was sent back to Holman & Moody for a strip-down and checking, which in the words of the *World Registry of Cobras and GT40s* 'was deja-vu all over again'! It included an engine rebuild in preparation for the 2004 Le Mans Classic. Lee Holman reported back: 'Only the piston rings need replacing, the pistons are fine but will need attention eventually. Everything else is in good condition.' New Goodyear tyres were fitted and the cracked windscreen changed, then the car was shipped

'After an extensive rebuild at Holman & Moody, 1016 started winning races, with its biggest success the US Vintage Grand Prix'

Renewed and back on track

- The theme for the 2003 Goodwood Festival of Speed was Ford's Centenary. The sculpture dwarfing Goodwood House celebrated the Blue Oval's 1-2-3 1966 Le Mans finish. The three cars were full-size replicas, not the multi-million dollar originals, but it was still jaw-dropping.

to Geneva, where it arrived on 7 May 2004.

After tests at Dijon (gentle) and Paul Ricard (hard) – where shock-absorbers and springs were replaced – Claude Nahum and Bernard Thuner shared 1016 at the July Le Mans Classic, but their weekend was ended by differential failure caused by an oil-feed problem. Claude's engineering expertise was to help him to identify and fix this and other later problems, and he now has a reliable race car.

In August 2004, 1016 was on show at the new Ford GT press launch at the French circuit of Anneau du Rhin (the closest track to Switzerland), and in 2006 it was back at Le Mans for Ford's 40th victory anniversary, where the three cars were lined up in their finish formation.

Then began another chapter in the 1016 story as Claude embarked on both race and concours programmes around the world, operating out of his Geneva workshop, run by Didier Burgisser's mechanic Trevor.

Mose Nowland

Mose Nowland was one of Ford's leading engine specialists, with a love for competition, a natural to work on the development of the 427 V8 into a twice Le Mans-winning engine, and on the small-block V8 which won the 1965 Indy 500 in the back of Jim Clark's Lotus.

A Ford employee all his working life, he was with the Engine & Foundry Division at Dearborn when Leo Beebe ordered the GT40 programme to change from Shelby 4.7 litre power to the big-block 7-litre Galaxie engines which Holman & Moody had been successfully using in NASCAR.

They were lightened at Engine & Foundry with alloy heads and other changes to make them better-suited for endurance racing on road circuits. He cites the Le Mans campaigns as his favourite times with Ford: 'Winning the 1966 and 1967 24 Hours of Le Mans with the GT40s in the presence of the Ford family, and how satisfied they appeared to be with our efforts, was special.

'The second most interesting experience was probably Indianapolis in 1963, 1964 and 1965 when we had the Ford-powered Lotus with Jim Clark and Dan Gurney. That was a very rewarding program because of the outcome, of course. We actually changed the style of racing and the style of the Indy 500 race car.'

Nowland was to work for the Blue Oval for an astounding 57 years, and was later involved with the company's rotary and small-block multi-fuel PROCO (Programmed Combustion) engine projects, neither of which was to go into production. He eventually 'retired' in 2012: 'I left the Foundry on Friday, and started at the Henry Ford Museum on the Monday'.

Five years later, Mose still keeps active as special consultant to the Dearborn museum – 'where Dan Gurney's 1967 Le Mans winning Mk IV resides, and which I get to see most days'. He also continues to advise on engine rebuild projects, including the 1964 small-block Indy V8 adapted for the GT40.

With Denis Mondrach of Ford Restoration Licencing and Performance Parts pointing him the right direction, Mose assisted Claude Nahum on the pushrod engine for his Ford GT/101 reconstruction, sourcing components that Claude needed, and using drawings he had kept to machine new parts; together with Curt Vogt, he delivered the jewel of a V8 which now powers the car, showing he has lost none of his magic touch.

Mose (right, in the picture) was Claude's guest at the 2015 Goodwood Revival, where he was a passenger in the car which he helped revive.

Renewed and back on track

- Appropriately, the Le Mans Classic in 2004 was 1016's first race in ownership of Claude Nahum and Bernard Thuner was first away from the traditional Le Mans start.
Claude Nahum collection

- Historic racing isn't always sun and roses: a proud moment for 1016's Turkish owner Claude Nahum as he wins in the murk at his home circuit of Istanbul at the 2005 historic festival, chased by a Porsche 917.
Claude Nahum collection

- There is night racing too, Claude in action again at the 2008 Le Mans Classic, the event held every two years in the month in following the 24 Hours.
Claude Nahum collection

Renewed and back on track

- ACO race director Daniel Poissenot raises his hat to the 1966 winning trio as the Ford Mk IIs re-enact their finish at the 2006 Le Mans Classic, the 40th anniversary of the Blue Oval's first victory. *Claude Nahum collection*

- Racing, concours events and motor shows all figure heavily in the calendar for Claude Nahum and 1016, which is rarely at its Geneva base during the season. Claude shares driving duties with his friend and mentor Bernard Thuner. *ICR/ JD Guillou*

Exceptional Cars

Renewed and back on track

2009 Festival of Speed and Claude powers 1016 up the Goodwood hill-climb, where the gold-and-pink No 5 Mk II has been a firm favourite with the crowds year after year.
Claude Nahum collection

Not only a race winner, but a show-stopper; here at the 2016 Pebble Beach Concours de'Elegance in California. 1016 is among 17 GT40s which gathered to celebrate the 1966 Le Mans win, against the backdrop of the Pacific Ocean.
Claude Nahum collection

Renewed and back on track

There it shares space with Claude's other cars: four GT40s (including a faithful replica of the long-gone first Ford GT prototype, and Mk IV chassis J-13), Cobras, Ferrari, Jaguar E-type, Lola T70, Mustang GT350, and more.

Trevor has a huge stock of spare parts, including a spare 1967 Mk IIB engine (with period twin 4-barrel Holley carbs) and a spare T-44 gearbox; the engines alternate in going to H&M every two years for rebuilds. The rear suspension was also reconditioned in 2005 by Bob Ash as part of ongoing servicing.

Claude Nahum's CV is exhausting – he has been racing 1016 every year since 2004 at the Le Mans Classic, Paul Ricard, Istanbul, Barcelona and Goodwood, and showing it at the Geneva Salon, Zaragosa, Angouleme, Villa d'Este, Chantilly, Le Castellet and Pebble Beach. In 2016 he and 1016 were at the 84th Le Mans 24 Hours for the 50th Anniversary of Ford's first win, where the theme was Americans at Le Mans.

- The concours at Villa d'Este, on the shores of Lake Como, rivals Pebble Beach for its beautiful cars; 1016 is there too and in 2011 won the Trofeo Auto & Design. Claude savours the moment in elegant company.
Claude Nahum collection

- 1016 is run out of Claude's Geneva workshop, tended by Trevor van Poppering. Here he gives last-minute to instructions to Claude before the 2016 Le Mans Classic.
Claude Nahum collection

Renewed and back on track

Post-1967 Historic Racing & Concours Appearances

This list is by no means exhaustive; 1016 has been seen at many races, concours and motor shows since it left Harrah's Motor Museum in 1983. These are the most notable

1981	Watkins Glen 2 Hours – 2nd Jacky Ickx/Brian Redman	2004	New Ford GT press launch, Anneau du Rhin, France
1993	Shelby American Automobile Club 18th Convention, Watkins Glen	2004-2016	Le Mans Classic
	(the first time that the three 1966 Le Mans Mk IIs had been reunited)	2005	1st GT Class, Istanbul
1993-1996	Historic races Elkhart Lake, Mid-Ohio – Ken, Darren and Brian Qunitenz		1st GT Class, Jarama
1966	Ford 30th Anniversary Gathering, Le Mans	2011	1st Trofeo Auto & Design, Villa d'Este
2001	1st Zippo US Vintage Grand Prix, Watkins Glen	2014	2nd Endurance, Chantilly Arts & Elegance
	Goodwood Festival		Geneva Salon
	Ford Racing Centennial, Dearborn	2016	Henry Ford II and Edsel Ford commemoration presentation Pebble Beach
2003	Ford Motor Company Centennial, Dearborn	2016	Ford victory 50th Anniversary, Le Mans
	Goodwood Festival Central Display		Baume et Mercier Show, Le Castellet
	People's Choice Award, Pebble Beach		

1016 squats down as Claude unleashes 500bhp of Detroit iron at the Goodwood Festival hill-climb. He has the choice of 1966 and 1967 V8s, mated to the Ford T-44 transaxle with which both Mk IIs and Mk IIBs ran. *Claude Nahum collection*

Renewed and back on track

Claude Nahum

A visit to the wonderland which is Claude Nahum's Geneva motorsport base says everything about this charming Turkish engineer and entrepreneur, whose passion is Le Mans cars. While most enthusiasts are content to collect model cars, Claude has not only the models, but the real ones too.

Ford GT40 P/1016, the subject of this book, is just one of dozens of sports cars – from Cobras to Jaguars, Ferraris to Lolas - which he has had restored and uses regularly, for pleasure, to race, or for show. 'Driving them is all about fun,' he says. 'Some people buy these cars as investments and never use them. I use mine all the time.'

Now 69, his love for cars was nurtured by his father Bernar, a pioneer of the Turkish automotive industry, who started out selling tractors in Anatolia in the late 1920s. Bernar later worked with the Koç Group in Ankara, of which he became president, and had the ear of both Fiat's Gianni Agnelli and Henry Ford II. Koç became Turkey's biggest car maker, producing Anadol cars and Otosan pick-ups, and entered partnerships with both Fiat and Ford, the latter's Istanbul plant producing the best-selling Transit van.

Whilst working for the company, Claude had considerable success rallying Anadol A1s with his brother Jan. He gained his MSc in the science of

● Claude Nahum at the office (left), awaiting a Le Mans Classic night race; among the few changes to 1016's 1966 spec is the Mk IIB aluminium instrument panel and H&M roll-cage. *Claude Nahum collection*

● Claude's automobile collection includes race cars, books and thousands of models, many of them of his beloved GT40s. These are exquisitely detailed scale models of six Ford Mk IIs from Le Mans 1966, including 1016 (no.5). *Claude Nahum collection*

Renewed and back on track

‘Some people buy these cars as investments and never use them. I drive mine all the time'

● Claude's biggest supporter has been his wife Sylvie; they are pictured together at the 2014 Chantilly Arts et Elegance in France, where 1016 was awarded second place in the Endurance concours.
Claude Nahum collection

engine induction before running the test cells for the 1973 California emissions standards at Ford's Dunton research establishment in the United Kingdom, and returning to Turkey to work in Anadol's research department. He was responsible for a prototype rotary engine which was far ahead of its time, although it never went into production due to high development costs, and he has it to this day.

Claude left the Koç Group in 1998 to plough his own furrow, and today is involved in many green enterprises, including the conversion of bio-waste into fertiliser – 'putting back into the soil what came from the soil,' as he describes it.

His car collection includes several GT40s, one of which is a reconstruction of the long-lost Ford GT/101 prototype which Schlesser destroyed at the 1964 Le Mans Test Weekend. He has 'reimagined' it, using as many original parts as possible. It is powered by an original Indycar V8, which Mose Nowland and Curt Vogt rebuilt for him.

Notable amongst his other cars are a Lola T70 – successfully raced by his long-time friend and racing mentor Bernard Thuner – and two Cobras, two Mustang GT350s and the Lang Cooper, nods to Shelby American. A Ferrari 250 GTO Favre reconstruction and a lightweight Linder/Nocker Jaguar E-type reconstruction by Lynx also sit in his Swiss race-shop, all looked after by Didier Burgisser's Burgol Team and his South African mechanic Trevor van Poppering, who crewed for Jacques Villeneuve in his British American Racing F1 days.

When pressed, he admits his favourite car is the ex-David Piper GT40 Mk 1 P/1078, with which Piper had much success. Claude has also won historic races with it – 'it fits me like a glove, when I drive it I am completely at home'. But Claude Nahum's philosophy is not the winning but the taking part - and the sheer pleasure of driving these icons.

Ford GT40 MkII 1016 | 113

Chapter 13
Photo gallery

Racing cars, like good claret, improve with age. But not all survive: Enzo Ferrari destroyed his F1 cars once they had done their job, saying that he had no further use for them.

Ford was also careless in the early days of the Ford GT40 project; the grandfather GT/101 was binned as having no value after crashing at the 1964 Le Mans tests. Fortunately, both Ferrari and Ford began to realise that these automobiles had history, and today the majority of the 100-plus GT40s – 24 prototypes and 86 production cars – built at Slough by FAV and JWAE live on.

Chassis P/1016 was delivered to Shelby American in California in late 1965 for upgrading to Mk II specification, with Ford's 7-litre V8 and T-43 transmission. For the next 18 months, during which it finished third at Le Mans, 1016 was also used as the factory test mule, gathering data which would help Ford to two Le Mans wins, ending Ferrari's six-year winning streak. It then became a Mk IIB, with further refinements.

Today, 1016 is fully restored and attracting attention, picking up race wins and show awards more than 50 years on. These specially-commissioned studio photographs by Pietro Bianchi and Mathieu Hertault present the car's beauty in detail, inside and out.

The all-important original chassis plate, confirming that this is indeed GT40 P/1016, affixed by Holman & Moody once the car had arrived at its Charlotte Municipal Airport base after an eight-day test at Sebring in January 1966.

Outwardly, Mk II 1016 appears today as it started the 1966 Le Mans 24 Hours, with the correct race number, decals and paint finish. Under the bodywork, a new dash, re-routed water pipes and a rear oil tank are among Mk IIB modifications.

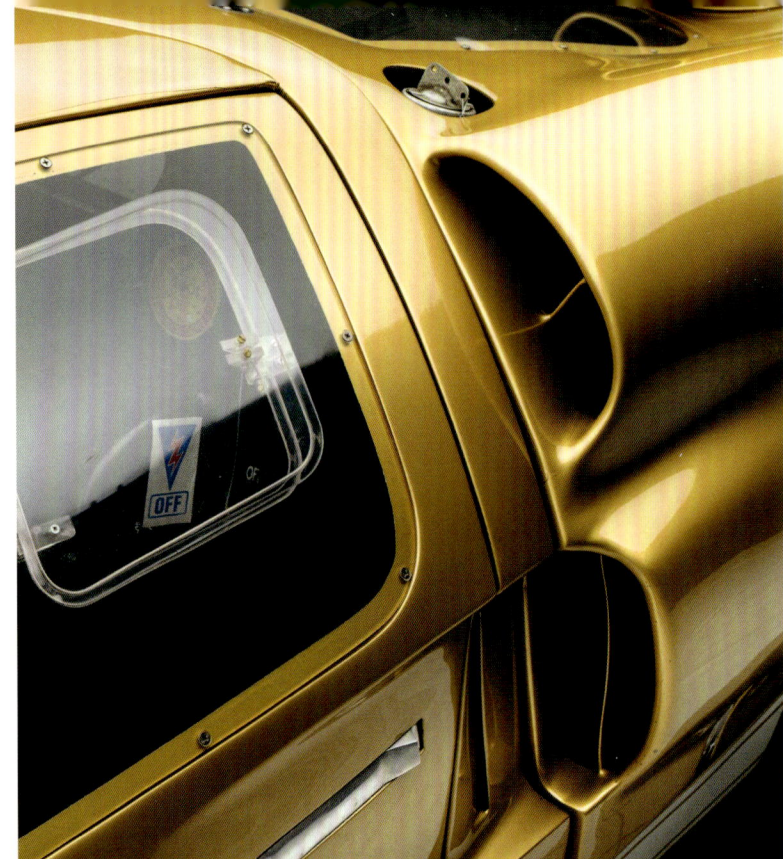

- The distinctive Len Bailey-designed slab nose was fitted to all GT40s from 1966, providing better front-end stability. Bigger air intakes behind the doors improved oil cooling; the rear-deck snorkels did the same for the brakes.

Ford production car parts were used where possible – rear lights among them. Note the adjustable rear spoiler. The H&M fire-extinguisher system, fitted where the oil tank used to bake the driver's feet, is a legacy from the Mk IIB.

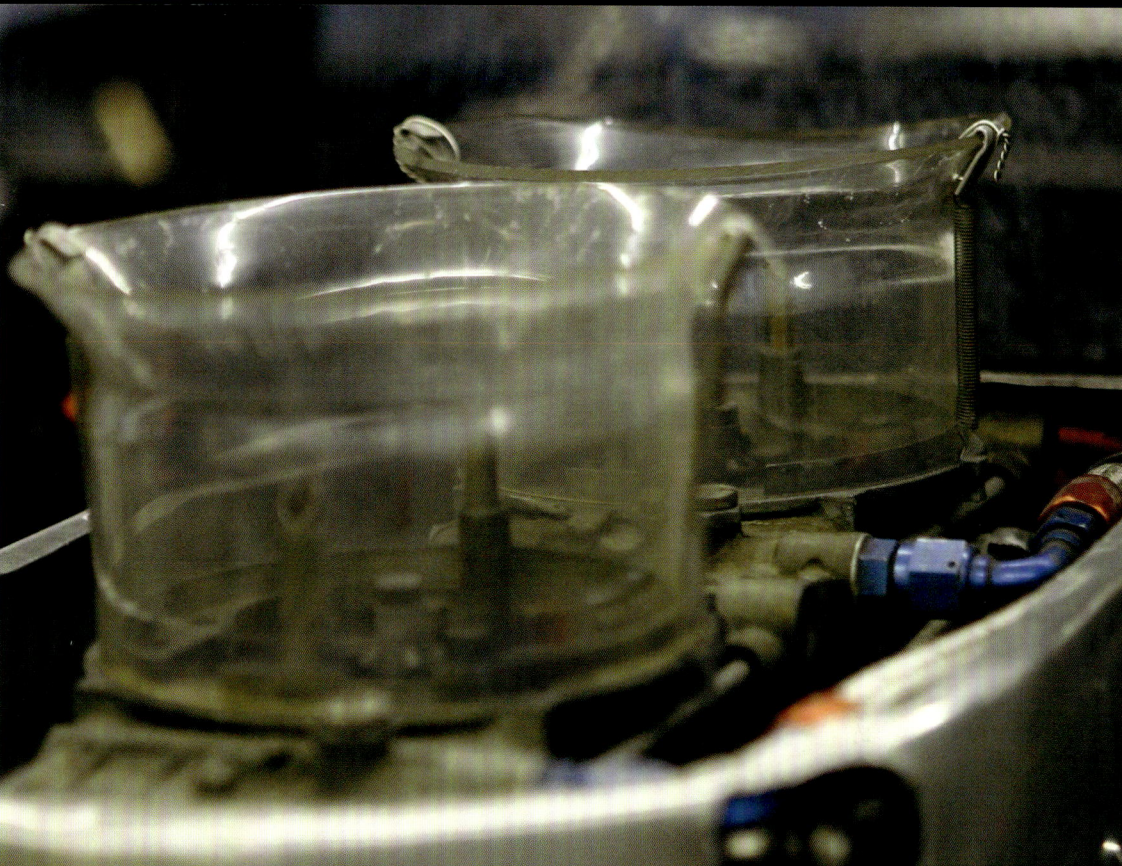

● The massive 7-litre V8 from the Fairlane in the back of 1016; this is the Mk IIB engine, with its twin 4-barrel Holley carburettors and 'snakepit' exhaust system. The Mk II V8 has a single Holley; Claude Nahum has both versions.

1016 started its competition life ● with Ford's T-43 auto transmission, but changed to T-44 four-speed manual for Le Mans 1966 after gearbox problems at both Daytona and Sebring. Note the Mk IIB oil tank and brake cooling ducts.

● The GT40 ventilation system was supposed to circulate through seat eyelets but never worked as it should have done. The aluminium dash in 1016 is a Mk IIB update, as is the passenger door to clear the H&M roll-cage.

As with all GT40s, 1016 is a right-hooker with the gearshift and its reverse block to the driver's right; the pedal box is moveable, rather than the seats. The modern rev counter red-lines the V8 at 6,500rpm, where it delivers 500bhp.

- Adjustable suspension was computer-designed at Dearborn, Halibrand cast magnesium wheels were part of Mk II specification and quick-change brake discs were a Holman & Moody development. Overheating brakes were the programme's Achilles heel, even with the move to ventilated discs.

Even after 50 years, the GT40 lines look timeless, and 1016's gold and pink colours show them off to their best. Doors open wide and cut deep into the roof to ease entry and exit. The side-pontoons house fuel tanks on each side.

Acknowledgements

My thanks to the many who helped me in uncovering both the story of 1016 and the Ford GT40 project, but in particular to:

Lindsay Morle, Ford Chip Ganassi Racing
Mose Nowland, Ford Engine & Foundry
Kevin Kennedy, Campbell Marketing & Communications
Dr János Wimpffen, Motorsport Research Group
And last, but not least, 1016 owner Claude Nahum

BIBLIOGRAPHY

Douglas Armstrong *Automobile Year 14* Edita 1964/65
Nate Adams & Adam Carolla *The 24 Hour War* Chassy Media 2016
AJ Baime *Go Like Hell* Bantam Books 2010
Gordon Bruce *Ford GT40 Owners' Workshop Manual* Haynes Publishing 2014
Brian Laban *Le Mans 24 Hours* Virgin Books 2001
Preston Lerner *Ford GT* Motorbooks/Quarto Publishing Group 2015
Quentin Spurring *Le Mans 1960-1969* Haynes Publishing 2010
János Wimpffen *Time and Two Seats* Motorsport Research Group 1999

Index

AC Ace 10, 12
Agnelli, Gianni 13, 112
Alan Mann Racing 30, 36, 39, 58, 65, 67, 70
Amon, Chris 29, 40, 45, 74, 71, 74, 81
Andretti, Mario 45, 56, 67, 70, 86, 90
Aston Martin 9, 10, 12, 14, 17, 18, 22, 23, 96
    DB2 14, 22
Attwood, Richard 19, 20
Bailey, Len 14, 23, 29, 32, 36
Bandini, Lorenzo 20, 54, 70, 81, 88
Beebe, Leo 20, 24, 26, 30, 70, 72, 105
Bianchi, Lucien 67, 70, 80, 81, 90
Bondurant, Bob 20, 26, 45
Bonnier, Jo 29, 40
Bordinat, Eugene 14, 76
Bowmaker Racing 14
BRM 46, 47, 86
Broadley, Eric 10, 14, 16, 18, 20, 23
Bucknum, Ronnie 40, 45, 47, 48-49, 50, 54, 56, 58, 64, 67, 68, 71, 72, 73, 74, 75
Buzzetta, Joe 45, 54
Can-Am 50, 76, 82, 85
Chantilly 95, 110, 111
Chaparral 26, 30, 32, 40, 47, 50, 78, 90
Chevrolet 10, 26
Corvette 10, 12, 54
Chinetti, Luigi 24, 29, 46, 48
Chrysler 10, 12, 75
Clark, Jim 28, 105
Cooper 14, 47, 48, 50, 113
Cunningham, Briggs 12, 16
Daytona 20, 24, 26, 27, 30, 32, 72, 86
    24 Hours 30, 35, 36, 38, 40-49, 50, 56, 76-85
    500 10, 12, 56
    Continental 2,000km 12, 24
Dearborn 12, 14, 16, 17, 20, 23, 27, 28, 32, 36, 38, 39, 81, 100, 105, 111
Donohue, Mark 38, 39, 40, 45, 50, 54, 58, 67, 68, 78, 81, 82, 84-85, 88, 86, 90
Drolsom, George 45, 81
Ferrari 7, 10-13, 14, 16, 19, 20, 22, 24, 26, 29, 39, 40, 46, 47, 48, 56, 58, 61, 67, 68, 70, 72, 76, 80, 88, 90, 92, 110, 112, 114
    250GTO 12, 113
    330P3 58, 65
    330P4 81, 88
    Dino 206P 54
    P4 76, 78
Fiat 13, 112
Filipinetti, Georges 28, 90
Ford (car) 7, 9, 13, 14, 24, 26, 29, 68, 80, 82
    Fairlane 10, 12
    Falcon 10, 30, 39
    France 29, 90
    Galaxie 10, 12, 26, 30, 65, 105
    GT 14, 16, 17, 19, 24, 32, 40, 76, 92, 104, 110, 111
    GT/**101** 105, 113
    GT40 7, 16, 17, 20, 22, 23, 24, 26, 27, 29, 30, 32, 35, 36, 50, 54, 58, 63, 70, 76, 81, 86, 90, 92, 96, 103, 105, 110, 113, 114
    Mk II 7, 23, 26, 28, 29, 30, 32, 35, 36, 38, 39, 40, 45, 48, 50, 54, 56, 58, 61, 65, 67, 70, 71, 72, 74, 75, 76, 78, 80, 81, 82, 84, 111, 114
    Mk IIB 39, 48, 56, 76, 78, 80, 81, 86, 88, 90, 96, 103, 110, 114
    Mk IV 7, 23, 32, 39, 48, 56, 81, 84, 86, 88, 90, 96, 105, 110
    Mustang 12, 16, 28, 82
    Mustang GT350 12, 110, 113
Ford (company) 7, 9, 10, 12, 13, 14, 16, 17, 20, 21, 22, 23, 24, 26, 27, 28, 29, 30, 32, 35, 36, 39, 40, 48, 50, 56, 58, 61, 65, 70, 72, 74, 75, 76, 78, 80, 84, 86, 88, 90, 92, 95, 96, 100, 104, 105, 110, 111, 112, 113, 114
Ford Advanced vehicles (FAV) 17, 20, 21, 23, 24, 27, 29, 30, 32, 35, 36, 39
Ford, Henry II "The Deuce" 7, 9, 10, 12, 29, 67, 111, 112
Formula **1** 12, 14, 29, 40, 46, 47, 48, 50, 82, 85, 86, 113
Foyt, Anthony Joseph 'AJ' 39, 48, 50, 54, 56-57, 58, 75, 81, 82, 86, 90, 92
Frey, Don 13, 14, 21, 73, 92
Gardner, Frank 58, 65, 70
Geddes, Ray 14, 22, 24
General Motors 10, 40
Ginther, Richie 19, 20, 26, 40, 45, 46-47, 48, 50
Goodwood 18, 82
    Festival of Speed 99, 100, 105, 110, 111

Tourist Trophy (TT) 22
Grand Prix,
    Italian 46, 48
    Mexican 40, 46, 48
    Monaco 46, 47
    Shelby Reunion Zippo US Vintage 100, 111
    United States 48
Grant, Jerry 40, 45, 72
Gregg, Peter 45, 54
Gregory, Masten 19, 20, 29
Grossman, Bob 54, 64
Gurney, Dan 20, 24, 39, 40, 45, 47, 50, 56, 64, 65, 67-71, 72, 78, 90, 92, 105
Hansgen, Walt 38, 40, 45, 50, 54, 58, 75, 84
Harrah's Automobile Collection 95, 96, 111
Hawkins, Paul 48, 67, 68, 84
Herrmann, Hans 45, 54, 74, 81
Hill, Graham 46, 65, 67, 70
Hill, Phil 12, 19-21, 29, 40, 46-47
Holman & Moody 7, 10, 26, 30, 32, 36, 39, 40, 47, 50, 58, 64, 67, 68, 70, 75, 76, 78, 84, 86, 88, 90, 92, 95, 96, 100, 103, 105
Honda 40, 46, 47, 48
Horsman, John 17, 23
Hull, Ed 76, 81
Hulme, Denny 71, 72, 74, 96
Hutcherson, Dick 48, 58, 64, 67, 71, 72, 73, 74, 75
Iacocca, Lee 10, 12, 17, 20
Ickx, Jacky 23, 81, 96, 111,
Indianapolis/Indy 12, 13, 16, 20, 105
    500 12, 28, 50, 56, 82, 85, 90, 105
Indycar 48, 56, 58, 75, 82, 113
Jaguar 9, 10, 112
    E-type 110, 113
JW Automotive Engineering (JWAE) 23, 96, 99, 114
Kar Kraft 27, 28, 30, 32, 76
Klass, Guenther 45, 74
Le Mans
    24 Hours 7, 8-13, 14, 16, 17,18, 19, 20, 22, 23, 24, 26, 27, 28, 29, 30, 32, 35, 39, 40, 46, 48, 50, 56, 58-74, 76, 84, 90, 92, 95, 96, 99, 100, 104, 105, 110, 111, 112
        Classic 103, 104, 110, 111
        Test Weekend 18, 28, 32, 39, 75, 86-89, 96, 113
Linge, Herbert 45, 74
Lola 10, 14, 16, 20, 112
    Mk6 GT 14, 16
    T70 20, 85, 110, 113
Lotus 10, 12, 16, 28, 84, 105
Lunn, Roy 14, 16, 18, 19, 20, 26, 27, 80
Maglioli, Umberto 29, 46
McLaren, Bruce 18, 19, 20-21, 26, 29, 39, 40, 45, 50, 56, 65, 68, 71, 73, 74, 80, 81, 82, 84, 85, 86, 88, 90
McQueen, Steve 23, 82

Miles, Ken 24, 26, 28, 29, 33, 36, 40, 45, 50, 54, 65, 67, 68, 70, 71, 72, 74, 76, 96
Milwaukee Mile 56, 58, 75
Mitter, Gerhard 45
Monza 14, 21, 46, 47
    1,000Km 58
Moody, Ralph 10, 39
Moss, Wes 39, 86
Motor Sport 17, 23, 46
Mountain, Chuck 14
Muir, Brian 65, 70
Nahum, Claude 7, 95, 100, 103, 104, 105, 110, 112-113
NART 24
NASCAR 10, 12, 30, 39, 48, 56, 58, 61, 75, 76, 105
Nassau Speed Week 21, 24
Nowland, Mose 105, 113
Nürburgring 22, 48
    1,000Km 19, 58
Parkes, Mike 58, 67, 81, 88, 90
Passino, Jacque 12, 30
Paul Ricard 104, 110
Pebble Beach 95, 100, 110, 111
Penske, Roger 23, 48, 82, 84, 85
Perry, Homer 30, 86
Porsche 9, 23, 48, 56, 65, 70, 85
    904 48
    904GTS 45, 54
    906 45, 54, 72, 74
    906LE 74, 81
    908, 82, 83
    908-3 23
    910 81
    911 81
    917 23, 48, 85
Quintenz, Ken 96, 100
Redman, Brian 96, 111
Remington, Phil 12, 24, 32, 80, 81
Revson, Peter 50, 54, 76, 78, 81, 82-83, 86
Rindt, Jochen 29, 45
Riverside 24, 30, 32, 58, 75, 76
Road America 95
Rodriguez, Pedro 24, 45, 48, 65, 68, 70, 81
Ruby, Lloyd 26, 45, 50, 54, 56, 58, 86, 90, 96
Salvadori, Roy 18, 19, 22
Scarfiotti, Ludovico 54, 70, 81, 90
Schlesser, Jo 18, 19, 90, 113
Schütz, Udo 45, 74
Scott, Skip 50, 54, 82, 86
Sebring 12 Hours 7, 12, 13, 17, 24, 26, 32, 35, 36, 38, 40, 46, 48, 50-55, 58, 64, 72, 76, 81, 82, 84, 86
Servoz-Gavin, Johnny 47
Shelby American Inc 7, 12, 22, 24-29, 30, 32, 35, 36, 38, 39, 40, 50, 58, 65, 67, 76, 78, 80, 81, 86, 90, 92, 96, 100, 113, 114

Shelby
    Cobra 10, 24, 40, 54, 84
    Cobra Daytona Coupe 10, 20, 24
    GT350 24, 74, 84
    GT40 24
    Mk II 7, 40
    Mk IIB 48
    Mk IV 86, 90
Shelby, Carroll 10, 12, 14, 22, 23, 29, 30
Smith, Carroll 12, 96
Spa 48
    1,000Km 58
Stewart, Jackie 58
Stutz 12
Surtees, John 14, 20, 24, 29, 48, 58, 88
Targa Florio 23
Thompson, Dick 65, 81
Thunier, Bernard 104, 113
TransAm 82, 85
Tucker, Jimmy 80, 99
Underwood, Lake 54
Villa d'Este 95, 110, 111
Voegele, Charles 54
Walker, Rob 28, 29
Wanderer, John 30, 32, 38, 39, 50, 80, 86, 88
Watkins Glen, 46, 111
    2 Hours 96
Whitmore, Sir John 21, 58, 67
Willment, John 23, 65
Willow Springs 24
World Sports Car Championship 12, 23
Wyer, John 7, 14, 16, 17, 18, 19, 20, 21, 22-23, 26, 29, 30, 32, 58, 90, 92
Yorke, David 23
Zimmerman, Frank 14, 16, 20